PRIMARY FOUNDATIONS

Geography

AGES 9-11

Wendy Garner and
Elaine Jackson

INTRODUCTION

Authors
Wendy Garner
Elaine Jackson

Editor
Gina Walker

Assistant Editor
David Sandford

Series Designer
Lynne Joesbury

Designer
Mark Udall

Illustrations
Beverly Curl

Cover photograph
Tony Stone Images

ACKNOWLEDGEMENTS

The publishers would like to thank:

ActionAid for use of material from their Chembakolli Pack, invaluable advice and help in the preparation of material with reference to the website www.chembakolli.com ActionAid, Chataway House, Leach Road, Chard TA20 1RR.

Material from the National Curriculum 2000 © The Queen's Printer and Controller of HMSO. Reproduced under the terms of HMSO Guidance Note 8.

Material from the Programmes of Study and *Geography: A Scheme of work for Key Stages 1 and 2* © Qualifications and Curriculum Authority 1998, 2000.

Published by Scholastic Ltd,
Villiers House,
Clarendon Avenue,
Leamington Spa,
Warwickshire
CV32 5PR
Visit our website at www.scholastic.co.uk
Text © 2000 Wendy Garner and Elaine Jackson; © 2000 Scholastic Ltd

3 4 5 6 7 8 9 0
2 3 4 5 6 7 8 9

3
Introduction

9
Chapter 1 – UK Localities
The local area
Contrasting localities

29
Chapter 2 – Economically Developing Countries
India – a land of many contrasts
Egypt – a land of surprises

49
Chapter 3 – Water and its Effects on the Landscape
Rivers
Coasts

71
Chapter 4 – Settlements
Investigating settlements
Using television to support the study of settlements

91
Chapter 5 – Environmental Change
Sustainablilty 'through the window'
What happens to all that waste?

112
Photocopiables

British Library Cataloguing-in-Publication Data
A catalogue record for this book is available from the British Library.

ISBN 0-439-01793-9

Introduction

About *Primary Foundations Geography*

Primary Foundations Geography suggests how geography can be divided into manageable teaching units for 9–11 year olds. Each themed chapter provides two units of work. These units are often complementary and so you could choose one or the other, or both, as appropriate to your needs.

Most of the units can be used to form the basis of a substantial amount of geography study – perhaps over a half term – and, by providing progressive lesson plans, show how geography can be sequenced.

The matrix at the beginning of each unit is intended to aid medium-term planning. Each one highlights (in bold) the key enquiry questions addressed by the lesson plans, as well as further questions to help you focus on the geographical aspects of the activity, or to extend the unit into other study areas. The matrices can also be used to help plan the cross-curricular links that geography has with other subjects – especially literacy, numeracy and ICT. The matrices will help with planning the resources that you need to collect in preparation for the unit of study that you choose.

The introduction to each unit provides background information that you may find useful when working with the lesson plans. Where necessary, further information is highlighted in the lesson plans themselves.

What is geography?

'Geography is a key part of the school curriculum because caring about the environment is essential to our survival. We must know how to make the best use, responsibly, of our resources and opportunities. Additionally, geography channels the natural human desire to understand how the world works – the processes and patterns that shape our lives, actions, places and environments.' *Simon Catling in* Handbook of Primary Geography, *ed. Roger Carter (Geographical Association 1998).*

The idea that geography is a subject where pupils learn the names and capital cities of different countries by rote is long outdated. As with other subject disciplines, geography has been shaped according to its perceived function in today's society and to some extent this is reflected in the revised National Curriculum for Geography (2000) where the notion of **environmental change and sustainable development** is identified as one of the key aspects of geography at primary level and beyond.

Geography is not only about developing a framework of locational knowledge, but is centrally concerned with helping children to develop the skills and understanding needed to be 'a geographer'. This actually means that the geographical skills and ideas children develop during the primary phase should be transferable to a wide range of different geographical contexts and issues.

Within the revised National Curriculum (2000), another key aspect of geography is identified as **geographical enquiry and skills** – a teaching and learning approach enabling children to ask, research and answer geographical questions about real places and environments. This enquiry-based method, which is actually transferable not only in terms of geographical content but also across different subject areas, firmly underpins the suggested activity ideas in this book. It is hoped that while this book helps teachers and pupils to engage in exciting geography, children will also develop their thinking skills and become more aware of how they learn.

The other two key aspects identified within the National Curriculum for Geography (2000) are **knowledge and understanding of places** and **knowledge and understanding of patterns and processes**.

These four aspects should run as strands through the study of the two localities and three themes specified in the National Curriculum for Geography (2000) in the Breadth of Study section

of the Programme of Study, and addressed in this book in five chapters broadly as set out in the table below.

Chapter	Breadth of Study section in Programme of Study
Chapter 1: UK Localities	'a locality in the United Kingdom' (6a)
Chapter 2: Economically Developing Countries	'a locality in a country which is less economically developed' (6b)
Chapter 3: Water in the Landscape	'water and its effects on landscapes and peoples' (6c)
Chapter 4: Settlements	'how settlements differ and change' (6d)
Chapter 5: Environmental Issues	'an environmental issue caused by change in an environment' (6e)

Links with the QCA Scheme of Work

Primary Foundations Geography closely relates to *A Scheme of Work for Key Stages 1 and 2* produced by the QCA in 1998. The units in this book link to specific units in the Scheme of Work and offer alternative ways in which they can be developed and delivered at short-term planning level, covering similar themes but using different teaching ideas.

The book as a whole covers all elements of the National Curriculum for Geography (2000). The table on page 8 can be used as a checklist to help you plan your own coverage of each Programme of Study statement through the units you select.

Numeracy links

In the new QCA unit 'Geography and Numbers', which was sent to schools during February 2000, geographical activities have been related to key aspects of the numeracy strategy. The activities taken from the Year 5–6 section have been reproduced below, as examples of possible numeracy links. You may want to integrate these ideas within units:

Key stage 2 (Y5–6)

Solving problems

● Ask the children to plan a route between two specific locations (for example, from their own street to a shopping centre in a nearby settlement) and to calculate distance travelled by car, bus, foot etc. (This may involve the use of a range of maps at different scales.) Ask the children to calculate total distance travelled in kilometres and then in metres.

Measures

● Ask the children to refer to a 1:50 000 Ordnance Survey map and to work out how many centimetres squared on the map equal one kilometre squared in real life. Children could then explore the area of different-sized settlements.

● Ask the children to use a world time chart to work out different times around the world. Transfer information to a display based on a map of the world.

Shape and space

● Ask the children to match photographs of river and coastal features to specific sites on an Ordnance Survey map using six-figure grid references.

● Revise the eight points of the compass. Ask the children to use a compass in conjunction with an Ordnance Survey map to describe a route.

Handling data

● Ask the children to study population data for two contrasting settlements and to produce a pie chart to illustrate proportions of the population within certain age groups. Calculate fractions and percentages and interpret/explain results using ICT where appropriate.

Literacy links

The introduction of the National Literacy Strategy, delivered through the Literacy hour is helping children develop the essential tools that are required to investigate the world in which they live, to develop their understanding of it, to record information about it, and to communicate what they have found out. The focus of geographical study is real places, both local and distant, and the relationships between these places and the people who live in them. Geography offers many exciting opportunities for children to engage in authentic language activities that have real purposes, audiences and outcomes. Teaching strategies and activities for delivering good geography involve the children in speaking, listening, reading and writing in all the six genres:

Forms of non-fiction writing that may be used to communicate responses to geographical enquiry questions	Examples of activities from the units of work in *Primary Foundations Geography*
Report genre – retelling events with the purpose of either informing or entertaining	● Compare and contrast transport used in rural and urban India. ● Compare transport used in India with modes of transport used in the UK. Write a report. ● Compare and contrast current land-use on the banks of a river with land-use shown on historical maps for the banks of the same river. Write a report identifying and explaining the major differences and changes.
Recount genre – describing the way things are	● Write about your visit to a landfill site.
Procedural/instructional genre – describing how something is done through a series of sequenced steps	● Write a recipe for a meal for an Indian banquet. ● Plan a journey from your school to Egypt. What sort of transport are you going to use and why? ● Plan what to pack for a visit to India in the monsoon season. ● Design a set of safety rules for a visit to a landfill site.
Explanation genre – explaining processes involved, or how something works	● Explain why it is necessary to follow a safety code when making a field visit to a landfill site
Discussion genre – presenting arguments and information from different viewpoints (for and against) before reaching a conclusion based on evidence	● In the role of a reporter attending a public meeting, write a report on the positive benefits and negative effects of the Aswan Dam on the lives of Egyptians for the 'Egyptian Daily News'. ● Set up an issue-based investigation about the siting of a landfill site in your local area. In role, debate the issues for and against the landfill site. Write a letter to the local council, putting forward reasons for and against the development.
Persuasion genre – promoting a particular point of view or argument	● Produce a travel brochure persuading people to go on different sorts of holidays to coastal areas in the UK – for example, beach holidays, rock climbing expeditions, birdwatching holidays. ● Make recommendations encouraging the use of more sustainable modes of transport (for example, more cycle lanes near school) and write to your local transport department trying to persuade the council to do something to help.

There is a wealth of both fiction and non-fiction books and materials available, which may be used to support geographical investigations and studies. Fiction books may be used to develop geographical skills, which may then be transferred to real-world investigations. Examples are given in the following table, linked to some of the chapters in this book.

Chapter	Fiction	Non-fiction
Chapter 2 Economically Developing Countries	● *The Day of Ahmed's Secret* by F Parry Heide and J Heide Gilliland (Gollancz 1991, ISBN 0 575 05132 9) ● *The Present* by Kopper and Bonnici (Mantra 1988, ISBN 1 852 69086 0) ● *The First Rain* by Kopper and Bonnici (Mantra 1984, ISBN 1 852 69065 8)	● *The Nile* by Julia Waterlow (Wayland 1992, ISBN 0 750 20428 1) ● *The Children of Egypt* by MA Pitkanen (Carolrhoda Books 1991, ISBN 0 876 14396 6)
Chapter 3 Water in the Landscape	● *River* by Charles Keeping (Oxford University Press 1978, ISBN 0 140 36913 9) ● *Where the River Begins* by T Locker (Patrick Hardy Books 1984, ISBN 0 744 40047 3) ● *The Wind in the Willows* by Kenneth Grahame (Puffin 1994, ISBN 0 140 36685 7)	● *Curriculum Visions – The River Book* by Dr B Knapp (Atlantic Europe Publishing 1998, ISBN 1 862 14005 7) ● *What Are... Rivers?* by A Owens (Heinemann First Library 1998, Big Book ISBN 0 431 02357 3; small book ISBN 0 431 02351 5) ● *Why Do We Have... Rivers and Seas?* by C Llewellyn (Heinemann 1997 ISBN 0 600 58691 X)
Chapter 5 Environmental Issues	● *The Iron Man* by Ted Hughes (Faber 1998, ISBN 0 571 13675 3) ● *The Iron Woman* by Ted Hughes (Faber 1999, ISBN 0 571 11716 X) ● *Dinosaurs and All That Rubbish* by M Foreman (Puffin 1974, ISBN 0 140 55260 X) ● *Shaker Lane* by A and M Provenson (Jula MacRae 1987, ISBN 0 862 03345 4)	● *Viewpoints on Waste* by R Martin (Heinemann Magic Bean series, 1998 ISBN 1 863 74052 X)

ICT links

Ways in which the following applications of ICT can be used effectively in geography are outlined in the lesson plans, and are highlighted on the planning matrices.

- CD-ROMs
- spreadsheets and data-handling software
- e-mail
- word-processing software
- digital cameras
- Internet

Useful websites

Geographical Association
www.geography.org.uk/home.htm

Primary Geographer Web Wizard
www.hope.ac.uk/ebs/webwizard/wizard.htm

QCA Schemes of Work (DfEE standards site)
www.standards.dfee.gov.uk/schemes/geography

Central Bureau for Educational Visits and Exchanges
www.wotw.org.uk

BBC (weather)
www.bbc.co.uk/weather

BBC Education – schools
www.bbc.co.uk/education/schools/

Intercultural e-mail Classroom Connections
www.stolaf.edu/network/iecc/

Eco-UK (environmental Internet links site)
www.eco-uk.com

Tidy Britain Group
www.tidybritain.org.uk

Going for Green/Eco-schools
www.gfg.iclnet.co.uk

Learning Through Landscapes
www.ltl.org.uk

Mersey Strategy
www.hope.ac.uk/ebs/merseystrategy/index.htm

Ordnance Survey
www.ordsvy.gov.uk/home/index.html

ActionAid
www.actionaid.org

Christian Aid
www.christian-aid.org.uk

Oxfam
www.oxfam.org.uk

Save the Children fund
www.oneworld.org/sfc

Useful Information

Publications and references

Handbook of Primary Geography ed. R Carter 1998, Geographical Association, Sheffield.
Geographical Enquiry at KS1–3: Discussion Paper Number 3. QCA 1998, London QCA.
Geography – A Scheme of Work for Key Stages 1 and 2. QCA 1998, London QCA.
Expectations in Geography at KS1 and KS2. SCAA (1997) London SCAA.

Programme of Study reference	Units in *Primary Foundations Geography*									
	The local area	Contrasting localities	India – a land of many contrasts	Egypt – a land of surprises	Rivers	Coasts	Investigating settlements	Using TV to support the study of settlements	Sustainability through the window	What happens to all that waste?
ask geographical questions (1a)										
collect and record evidence (1b)										
analyse evidence and draw conclusions (1c)										
understand different points of view (1d)										
communicate in different ways (1e)										
use geographical vocabulary (2a)										
use fieldwork techniques and instruments (2b)										
use atlases and globes, and maps and plans (2c)										
use secondary sources of information (2d)										
draw plans and maps (2e)										
use ICT (2f)										
decision-making (2g)										
identify and describe places (3a)										
locate places and environments (3b)										
describe where places are (3c)										
explain why places are like they are (3d)										
investigate change in places (3e)										
compare places (3f)										
wider contexts and interdependence (3g)										
recognise and explain patterns (4a)										
recognise physical and human processes (4b)										
people, environments and the future (5a)										
managing environments sustainably (5b)										
investigate a UK locality (6a)										
investigate a contrasting locality overseas (6b)										
investigate water and its effects on landscapes and people (6c)										
investigate settlements (6d)										
investigate an environmental issue (6e)										
local scale (7a)										
regional scale										
national scale										
range of places – UK (7b)										
range of places – EU										
range of places – rest of the world										
fieldwork investigations (7c)										

Remember, *A Scheme of Work for Key Stages 1 and 2* produced by the QCA in 1998 only represents examples of possible medium-term planning units. This book allows you to develop and complement those units in a flexible way to meet the needs of your children and your school.

UK Localities

Introduction

The revised National Curriculum for Geography (2000), in the Breadth of Study section of the Programme of Study, specifies that at least one UK locality is studied at Key Stage 2 (6a). This locality does not have to be the school's local area; it can be any locality within the United Kingdom. However, it is strongly recommended that teachers consider a flexible approach with regard to this requirement, possibly combining some aspects of local area study with work on a contrasting locality within the UK. This ensures that the potential and importance of local area work is not overlooked and that children have the opportunity to develop an awareness and understanding of contrasts within the UK.

The two units of work in this chapter are called 'The local area' and 'Contrasting localities'. The lesson plans described for these two units (pages 11 and 20) offer ideas and strategies for local area work, and for work on contrasting UK localities. Teachers may select appropriate lessons from the two units and combine them to make a single 'unit' that suits the needs and experiences of their school. For example, in a city school, teachers might create a unit by combining some local area work with a village study (where a village is visited as part of the Year 6 residential experience/ PSHE curriculum). This is possible because 'The local area' offers generic strategies for local area work and can be tailored to fit your own locality, and 'Contrasting Localities' offers alternative strategies depending on the settlement type of the contrasting locality being studied (this would be a village in the context of the stated example).

One of the main aims of a combined unit such as this would be to offer opportunities for children to compare and contrast localities, to identify similarities and differences between their locality and one other (which will probably be in the same country as their own).

If curriculum time is heavily constrained, however, then it is advisable to choose the local area study rather than the contrasting UK locality for the following reasons:

- the local area is relevant to, lived in and used by children in the school
- local area work enables children to build on their developing spatial awareness
- local area work is usually safe, free and accessible
- local area work helps children to develop the skills and confidences needed to study more distant localities that can probably never be visited (for example, 'Economically Developing Countries', page 29).

If your school does choose to focus on the local area but not a contrasting one, then remember that the thematic study of settlements requires children to study a number of contrasting places (see 'Settlements', page 71) and a more representative view of the UK might be built up within this context.

The four aspects of geography, as specified in the National Curriculum Programme of Study, can be taught through the study of a UK locality:

- **Geographical enquiry and skills** – for example, children analyse evidence and draw conclusions, by comparing population data for two localities.
- **Knowledge and understanding of places** – for example, children describe and explain how and why places are similar to and different from other places.
- **Knowledge and understanding of patterns and processes** – for example, children recognise and explain patterns made by human features in the local area, such as the distribution of different land-uses.
- **Knowledge and understanding of environmental change and sustainable development** – for example, children recognise how and why people may seek to manage environments sustainably.

The local area

Background information

The local area of each school is unique and will offer its own range of geographical features. The following will help you develop a resource and knowledge base specific to your area.

- **Photographs** – take a range of photographs of physical and human features in the area; try to obtain views that the children may not have seen or have access to.
- **Maps** – an Ordnance Survey 'Landranger' map is a good starting point as it will give you a feel for the overall site and situation of the area you are studying. Street maps and tourist maps are useful too as they show the spatial distribution of different aspects at a range of scales.
- **Aerial photographs** – these will help identify the overall shape and main features of the area.
- **ICT** – the 'Local Studies' software (*Mapping Skills* from Soft Teach Educational) is an excellent package for local area work as children can produce maps, scan images and compile texts to build up a detailed view of their locality.
- **Historical documents** – your local record office can provide a range of useful historical documents such as trade directories, census returns, and archival maps.
- **Planning documents** – local planning offices are often keen to involve schoolchildren in planning proposals and may offer resources such as aerial views, maps and other important information relating to specific sites in the local area.
- **Local newspapers** – local papers may help with the identification of local issues and people's responses to such issues.
- **Visiting speakers** – an extremely useful resource is a visiting speaker; for example, someone who has lived in the area for a considerable period of time.

Sustainable development

During the lessons described for this unit, children study their local area and consider, among other things, how it is changing. They look at the effects of various activities, and consider the environmental issues that arise from these activities.

Sustainable development is centrally concerned with reducing pressure on the environment caused by human activities, protecting all forms of wildlife, promoting the wiser use of resources and reducing pollution. Agenda 21 represents a global plan of action for the 21st century (established at the Rio Summit, 1992) and embraces the key principles of sustainable development. The 'Local Agenda 21' initiative has been implemented at local authority level and the following eight key themes have been identified:

- **transport** – aiming to encourage the use of more sustainable modes of transport
- **energy** – aiming to decrease the use of household and commercial energy
- **land-use** – aiming to decelerate the process of urbanisation and outward growth
- **water** – aiming to avoid waste and to improve the quality of natural water systems
- **air** – aiming to reduce the level of air pollution
- **waste** – aiming to reduce waste, to reuse materials and to recycle
- **wildlife** – aiming to maintain and promote diversity
- **landscape** – aiming to maintain and promote diversity of plants and trees in particular.

These themes cover various forms of legislation relating to environmental sustainability. Many have been drawn up by the Environment Agency, and may affect industries in the local area.

In the final lesson in this unit, children prepare and carry out a mock public inquiry about a local planning development with various social, political, economic and environmental implications. Ideally, this should be a real local land-use issue, so it may be a good idea to build up a display showing newspaper articles on local land developments and plans or pictures of proposals from the local planning office from the beginning of the unit. Children could help collect and display this information, and will therefore become familiar with it and the issues surrounding it as they go along. They will then be better prepared to select and discuss an issue when it comes to the final lesson.

UNIT: The local area

Enquiry questions	Teaching objectives	Teaching activities	Learning outcomes	Cross-curricular links
Where are we? How would a visitor from another country get to our local area from the airport?	• Communicate in ways appropriate to the task and audience. • Use appropriate geographical vocabulary. • Use atlases, globes, maps and plans at a range of scales. • Use secondary sources of information. • Draw plans and maps. • Learn about a UK locality. • Locate the places and environments studied.	In groups, children use photocopiable pages 112 and 113 to locate their local area and to develop an awareness of their place within the local, regional, UK, European and global context. Children imagine a visitor is arriving from a land of their own choice at a major airport. They write a travel itinerary to enable the visitor to get from the airport to their own locality. Children must think about best mode of transport, as well as the route, using secondary sources as appropriate.	Children: • can locate the local area on maps at a range of scales • can use secondary sources of information to plan a route to their local area	Numeracy: calculation of distance and time of journey.
What is our local area like? What are the main human and physical features of our local area?	• Collect and record evidence. • Analyse evidence and draw conclusions. • Communicate in ways appropriate to the task and audience. • Use appropriate geographical vocabulary. • Use appropriate fieldwork techniques. • Use atlases, globes, maps and plans. • Use secondary sources of information. • Learn about a UK locality.	On photographs of the locality, children annotate human and physical features. In groups, children list the main features that characterise their locality using the photographs and prior knowledge. Children walk a trail and take photographs of human and physical features that characterise their local area. Children mark the route taken onto a map and use a compass to orientate themselves. Through discussion, children compare field experiences with the lists of features they made earlier from prior knowledge and secondary sources. As a class, children produce a collage of fieldwork evidence (photographs, written commentary) to include a map of the route taken.	• develop awareness and understanding of the main features of the local area • can use a map and a compass to orientate themselves whilst following a trail	
What is our settlement like? What type of settlement do we live in? Why did people settle here originally? What are the main land-uses today? How and to what extent has our settlement changed?	• Collect and record evidence. • Analyse evidence and draw conclusions. • Communicate in ways appropriate to the task and audience. • Use appropriate geographical vocabulary. • Use and atlases, globes, maps and plans. • Use secondary sources of information. • Learn about a UK locality.	Children use historical documents, maps, photographs and census evidence to find out about the origin of the whole settlement. They record their findings on photocopiable page 114. Using aerial photographs of their settlement, children produce land-use data and a map using photocopiable page 115. As a class, children discuss current economic activities in the settlement. They compare this with the evidence of past activities, and relate it to land-use and the shape of the settlement recorded earlier. Children discuss the extent to which the settlement has grown/ declined and the nature of such changes.	• begin to understand the origins of their settlement. can use aerial photographs to identify shape and land-use in a settlement • begin to understand how and why settlements change	
How do different activities affect our settlement? What are the effects of local industry? What type of pollution is evident? What might be the environmental issues of the future?	• Ask geographical questions. • Collect and record evidence. • Analyse evidence and draw conclusions. • Use appropriate geographical vocabulary. • Use appropriate fieldwork techniques. • Draw maps and plans. • Use ICT to help in geographical investigations. • Learn about a UK locality. • Recognise how people can improve the environment or damage it. • Recognise how decisions about places and environments affect the quality of people's lives.	Children study the effects of local economic activities on the environment; for example, by going on a field visit to parts of the local area, including an industrial site, for observation, recording, photography and field sketching. Children identify different types of pollution (eg physical, visual, noise), in different parts of the local area (eg industrial, retail, farming, residential), and record their findings on photocopiable page 116. Back in class, children analyse and present their findings using spreadsheets and graph-drawing packages. Children predict what the economic activities and possible environmental issues in the local area might be in the future, and identify evidence of change on maps.	• develop awareness of different types of pollution	ICT: use of spreadsheets to present and analyse data.
Which places do I like in the local area? Which places do I like most or least, and why? What is the main land-use issue in the local area? What views do people hold and why?	• Use appropriate geographical vocabulary. • Use appropriate fieldwork techniques. • Use atlases, globes, maps and plans. • Use secondary sources of information. • Use decision-making skills. • Learn about a UK locality. • Recognise how people can improve the environment or damage it. • Recognise how decisions about places and environments affect the quality of people's lives. • Locate the places and environments studied. • Identify and explain different views that people, including themselves, hold about topical geographical issues.	Children study their local area through personal experience, maps and photographs, and identify desirable and less desirable features. Children give reasons for their preferences, and learn to appreciate that other people have other preferences. Choose a particular land-use issue from an ongoing 'Newsboard' of articles and information about local developments and planning proposals. Organise a mock public inquiry where children present different people's viewpoints in role. Children vote on a possible outcome.	• can identify what they like and dislike in the local area. begin to understand why different people hold different views about the same land-use issue.	Literacy: speaking and listening in role Citizenship: appreciating and tolerating vies held by others.

Resources
Copies of photocopiable pages 112–116; copies of page 115 on acetate; maps including local area, at a range of scales; photographs and aerial photographs of local area; cameras; field trail map constructed from local street map; compasses; historical documents on the origin of the local settlement; access to computer, scanner and software (word-processing, spreadsheets or graph-drawing packages, image manipulation software).

The local area

 Where are we?

Learning objectives
● Communicate in ways appropriate to the task and audience.
● Use appropriate geographical vocabulary.
● Use atlases, globes, maps and plans at a range of scales.
● Use secondary sources of information.
● Draw plans and maps.
● Learn about a UK locality.
● Locate the places and environments studied.

Lesson organisation
Initial teacher-led discussion with whole class, followed by group work on photocopiable pages 112 and 113, and then paired work; whole-class plenary session at the end.

Vocabulary
Depends on features of your local area, but may include:
locality
settlement
region
country
United Kingdom
continent
Europe
route
transport
distance
direction
grid references

What you need and preparation
You will need: copies of photocopiable pages 112 and 113 (one copy of each per child); street map of local area and pins; maps showing the locality, the region, the country, the continent, the world; a globe; an atlas; Ordnance Survey map showing an airport; airport flight arrival times; rail timetable and prices; bus timetable and prices; taxi fare quotations.

What to do

10 mins Introduction
Involve the children in developing a display using the street map of the local area. They should locate where they live using mapping pins. Introduce the lesson to the whole class using the display.
● What proportion of children in the class live in the immediate locality of the school?
● How many children live further away?
● Where do they live?
● What are the main features of the local area?
● What is the position/significance of the local area within the whole settlement? (If the settlement is a village, the school area may be highly significant; if the school is in a city suburb, however, the local area may constitute just a small part of the settlement.)
    Explain to the children the focus of the lesson:
● to develop awareness of where the local area is
● to be able to direct a visitor to the local area using a range of mapping skills
● to work effectively in groups.

1 hour Development
Ask the children to work for 20 minutes in groups of about four to complete photocopiable pages 112 and 113, locating the local area at a range of scales.
    Brainstorm as a whole class what a travel guidebook would need to have in it to help a visitor to find their way to the local area from the nearest airport. For example, it needs to have details about modes of transport, cost, timetables, distances, directions and alternative routes (such as direct or scenic).
    Ask the children to work in pairs to produce a travel itinerary (which should include a map) for a visitor landing at the nearest large airport (for example, Manchester, Heathrow or Birmingham airports). They should use the points that came out of the brainstorm as a basis from which to begin.

10 mins Plenary
Discuss the children's draft travel itineraries:
● Of all the routes planned by the class, which route is shortest? Which is longest? Which is cheapest, and which most expensive? Which route do they think is the most scenic?
● Which route has the quickest journey time? Which has the longest journey time? To what extent is this affected by the mode of transport?
● Which places of interest in the local area would the children recommend to their visitor?

Differentiation
Less able children may be given teacher support on using map scales and grid references during the activity.

More able children may be asked to produce a proposal for the return journey, which may extend over more than one day; children should suggest possible stopping points and a schedule of places of interest.

Assessing learning outcomes

Ephemeral evidence
● Children's use of mapping skills – use of scale and grid references.

Retainable evidence
● Children's itineraries, which evidence mapping skills (using and making maps) and a developing framework of locational knowledge.

ICT opportunities
Children could use the 'Local Studies' software (*Mapping Skills* produced by Soft Teach Educational, ISBN 0 948808 17 9) to produce maps of the proposed route from the airport to the local area. They could then use their maps as covers for their itineraries to produce 'travel guide' booklets.

Follow-up activity
Having discussed their itineraries, children could go on to produce final versions, perhaps combining with other groups to produce a larger booklet offering a range of different journey options.

 # What is our local area like?

What you need and preparation

You will need: a set of six enlarged (A4) photographs, each showing different features of the local area (show a balance of human and physical features – use the Vocabulary list below as a guide); compasses; copy of a route map for each child (which you could develop from a commercial street map); six sheets of acetate per group; acetate pens (six of one colour, and six of another – one pair for each group); writing materials for each group; cameras and film for each group; parents or other volunteers to help supervise the field trip; access to a computer and scanner; display materials.

Carry out a risk assessment for the field activity, and have a first aid kit available in the field.

As children will be working in six groups on the classroom-based activity, ensure you have identified these groups ahead of time.

Learning objectives
● Collect and record evidence.
● Analyse evidence and draw conclusions.
● Communicate in ways appropriate to the task and audience.
● Use appropriate geographical vocabulary.
● Use appropriate fieldwork techniques.
● Use atlases, globes, maps and plans.
● Use secondary sources of information.
● Learn about a UK locality.

Lesson organisation
Initial teacher-led discussion with whole class, followed by group work (in classroom, and then field-based); whole-class plenary session at the end.

What to do

Introduction
10 mins Introduce the lesson to the whole class by brainstorming examples of physical and human features. These may include houses (residential areas), shops (retail), industry (manufacturing, service), water features (rivers, coasts) and relief (hills, mountains, flood plains and so on).

Explain the focus of the lesson:
● to develop understanding of the differences between human and physical features
● to develop field techniques, such as using a map and a compass
● to develop knowledge and understanding of the main features in the local area.

Vocabulary
Depends on features offered by your local area, but may include:
river
relief
slope
stream
housing
residential
shops
retail
industry
manufacturing
school
church
transport networks

The local area

Development
Part 1: classroom-based activity (30 minutes)

● Give each of the six groups one of the enlarged photographs of local features. Ask each group to spend five minutes identifying human and physical features, and labelling them on a blank sheet of acetate over the photograph, using two coloured acetate pens. (They should use one colour for human features and the other for physical features.)

● Ask the children to start lists of physical and human features on a separate sheet of paper. Then they should keep their acetate, and pass their photograph on to the next group to look at. When they receive a new photograph from the previous group, they use a fresh acetate to label the features as before. This should be repeated six times, so that each group has a chance to view each photograph.

Part 2: field-based activity (1 hour)

● Provide each child with a map of the local area, marked with the positions of various human and physical features. Ask all the children, in small groups, to work out a route that they could follow to visit each of these features. The children should plot the route on their own copy of the map, and then follow the route in groups, using a compass when necessary.

● Ask each group to photograph and make notes to describe the main physical and human features they visit on their route (one photograph at each stopping point).

● On return to class, ask the children to compare their field notes with the lists of the main features that they made earlier, from their own knowledge and secondary sources of information.

Plenary
As a whole class, produce a list of the main human and physical features of the local area. Discuss the location of such features and why they might be where they are.

Differentiation
The groups should be chosen so that children of different abilities work together.

Assessing learning outcomes
Ephemeral evidence
● Children's discussion of the human and physical features.

Retainable evidence
● Children's original lists of features and field evidence (photographs and maps).

ICT opportunities
Children could scan the photographs taken in the field and use appropriate software to manipulate and annotate them for display.

Follow-up activity
The children could produce a display of their field-based evidence, to include their photographs with annotations and written commentary, based on a large-scale plan of the local area that shows the routes they took on their field trails.

What is our settlement like?

Learning objectives
● Collect and record evidence.
● Analyse evidence and draw conclusions.
● Communicate in ways appropriate to the task and audience.
● Use appropriate geographical vocabulary.
● Use atlases, globes, maps and plans.
● Use secondary sources of information.
● Learn about a UK locality.

What you need and preparation
You will need: sand tray containing a mixture of sand and gravel; watering can with rose; historical documents on the origins of your settlement (trade directories, census data, 'Doomsday' extracts, archival maps and photographs); oblique and vertical aerial photographs of settlement for each pair; copies of photocopiable pages 114 and 115 for each child; photocopiable page 115 copied onto acetate for each pair; acetates and acetate pens of different colours for each pair.

What to do
Introduction
Introduce the lesson to the whole class, possibly by demonstrating what the physical profile of the local region might have looked like before humans settled there, using a sand

The local area

tray and watering can. Using a watering can with a rose, gently sprinkle 'rain' onto the mixture of sand and gravel representing the 'land', so that the running water causes erosion and deposition, and creates features similar to those of the physical landscape of the region. Emphasise that might have been what the area looked like in the past, *before* humans settled there. Briefly discuss possible reasons for the settlement developing where it has.

Explain to the children the focus of the lesson:
● to investigate the origins of their settlement within the region
● to explore reasons for its growth or decline
● to locate their local area within the context of the whole settlement.

10 mins Development
Ask the children to investigate, in pairs, the origins of their settlement using a range of historical documents and to communicate their findings in the form of a report from a 'detective' (using photocopiable page 114).

Now ask the children, in pairs, to look at a vertical aerial photograph of the whole settlement; that is, a view from directly above the ground, showing the way the settlement is spread over the land, in two dimensions. The children should sketch the overall shape of the settlement.

Next, the children should place an acetate copy of photocopiable page 115 over the aerial view and trace the shape of the settlement onto the gridlines. Ask them to shade different parts of the settlement area using different coloured acetate pens, according to land-use (the classifications are fairly arbitrary, but you could use, for example: residential, industrial, retail, tended open space, public buildings, water features). Show children the outline of their local area (based on where the majority of the children live, shop and play) and its location with respect to the whole settlement.

Ask the children now to copy the outline and shaded areas from the acetate onto their own paper copies of photocopiable page 115 as accurately as possible. They should draw a key to show which colours represent which land-uses. Next they should devise a way of calculating land-use proportions; for example, by counting up the number of squares in each colour, and then using this data to produce a pie chart.

20 mins Plenary
As a whole class, discuss what has been found out about the origins of the settlement.
● Why did people originally settle here?
● Are other sources of evidence needed to complete the enquiry?

Next, discuss the main land-use proportions and relate them to the functions of the settlement in the past and present.
● What was/is the function of the settlement in the past/today? (For example, is it a port, a resort, a market town or based on another industry such as mining or manufacturing?)
● How has this function affected land-use?

Differentiation
Less able children could produce a colour-coded land-use plan for the second activity, which they annotate with labels provided by the teacher (such as 'roads', 'houses', 'river'). They may then simply list the three main land-uses by estimation (rather than by calculation).

Assessing learning outcomes
Ephemeral evidence
● Discussion when children relate their findings to growth/decline and change in their settlement.
Retainable evidence
● 'Detective' reports on the origins of the settlement, and land-use data and presentation.

Lesson organisation
Brief initial teacher-led discussion with whole class, followed by paired work on photocopiable pages 114 and 115, which form the basis of a whole-class plenary session at the end.

Vocabulary
Depends on features offered by your local area, but may include:
settlement
hamlet
village
town
city
conurbation
nucleated
linear
dispersed
land-use
economic activity
commercial
retail
industrial

ICT opportunities
Children could use spreadsheets and data-handing packages to organise and present their land-use data using percentages, graphs or pie charts, for example.

Follow-up activity
Children could contribute to a whole-class papier mâché model or display of their settlement, showing major features and land-uses.

The local area

4–5 hours How do different activities affect our settlement?

Learning objectives
- Ask geographical questions.
- Collect and record evidence.
- Analyse evidence and draw conclusions.
- Use appropriate geographical vocabulary.
- Use appropriate fieldwork techniques.
- Draw maps and plans.
- Use ICT to help in geographical investigations.
- Learn about a UK locality.
- Recognise how people can improve the environment or damage it.
- Recognise how decisions about places and environments affect the quality of people's lives.

Lesson organisation
Children work for half a day on field-based tasks (using photocopiable page 116) and then take turns, in small groups, to analyse and present their findings using ICT; whole-class plenary session when completed.

Vocabulary
environment
sustainability
industrial
pollution
economic activities
energy
waste
water
landfill sites
landscape

What you need and preparation
You will need: access to a local industrial estate, or ideally several areas in which different kinds of industry are dominant; one copy photocopiable page 116 for each child per area visited; clipboard, pens and paper for each child; cameras and film; access to computers with spreadsheet software.

What to do

10 mins Introduction
Introduce the lesson to the whole class through discussion of Agenda 21 (see 'Background information' on sustainable development, on page 10, and also page 91 in Chapter 5, 'Environmental Change'). Explain how legislation related to Agenda 21 affects industry.
Explain to the children the focus of the lesson:
- to collect and record field evidence relating to industrial activity and environmental issues
- to analyse and communicate in ways appropriate to the task and audience.

4 hours Development
Part 1: field-based activity (about 3 hours)
- Visit parts of the local area where different economic activities dominate, including an industrial site. For example, you could visit an industrial estate or factory, a farm or market garden, a retail area, a business district with office buildings, a residential area, or even perhaps an airport. Ask the children to use photocopiable page 116 to record their own appraisal of the environment in terms of how it looks, noise pollution and any other pollution that is evident. They should make sketches and notes in the spaces available to record their ideas, thoughts and feelings about the area, and 'rate' it in terms of each aspect (aesthetics/noise/pollution) on a scale of 1 to 3, by circling one of the numbered comments. They should consider aspects of the whole environment, including surrounding roads, pavements or green areas, and complete a separate sheet for each area visited.
- Ask the children to take photographs too, as another way of recording their findings visually.
- On return to school, in a whole-class discussion, briefly relate the children's findings to the introductory discussion of how environmental legislation affects local industrial activities.

Part 2: computer-based activity in small groups (rotating) (1 hour)
- Ask children to organise and present their findings from the field-based activity, as recorded on photocopiable page 116, using spreadsheets and graphs on the computer. For example, they could produce pie charts showing the collective responses of the class to each location. They should aim to demonstrate any relationships they find between the main type of industry in the area and the nature of the environment. (Clearly, the more different locations the children are able to visit, the more data they will have to analyse, and the more obvious any relationships will be.)

10 mins Plenary
Discuss what might happen to the areas looked at during the field study in the future, in terms of the types of economic activities that might occur there and the nature of the environmental issues surrounding those activities. For example, an area might experience increased urbanisation, pollution or traffic problems as a result of increased industrial activity. On the other hand, an area may become run-down or derelict if economic activity slows down. Children should work in mixed-ability groups during both fieldwork and on computer-based tasks.

Differentiation
Children should work in mixed-ability groups during both fieldwork and computer-based tasks.

Assessing learning outcomes
Ephemeral evidence
● Discussion of pollution indicators in the field.
Retainable evidence
● Field notes on photocopiable page 116, and computer-generated graphs that illustrate findings.

ICT opportunities
Children can use data-handling software, such as spreadsheet and graph-drawing packages, to analyse and present their fieldwork findings.

Follow-up activity
Ask the children to invite representatives from local industry into school, with a view to interviewing them on environmental legislation and the measures their companies have to take.

(2 hours) Which places do I like in the local area?

What you need and preparation
It is important that children appreciate that different people may have different views towards the same land-use issue. It may be useful to consider the following perspectives when working with the children to prepare for the mock public inquiry about a chosen local development proposal:
● **Social** – how will the proposal affect the community?
● **Political** – what are the political interests of those for and against the proposal?
● **Economic** – what money-making potential does the proposed site have?
● **Ecological** – what animals and plants are there on the proposed site, and what do they need to survive?

Remember that this form of 'public inquiry' activity links in with citizenship and the new requirements of the National Curriculum (2000).

You will need: 'Newsboard' display showing newspaper articles about local land developments and plans or pictures of proposed developments from the local planning office; a wide range of photographs of the local area, some of which depict changing land-use and highlight environmental issues; costumes and other props for the local 'public inquiry' debate.

Learning objectives
● Use appropriate geographical vocabulary.
● Use appropriate fieldwork techniques.
● Use atlases, globes, maps and plans.
● Use secondary sources of information.
● Use decision-making skills.
● Learn about a UK locality.
● Recognise how people can improve the environment or damage it.
● Recognise how decisions about places and environments affect the quality of people's lives.
● Locate the places and environments studied.
● Identify and explain different views that people, including themselves, hold about topical geographical issues.

Lesson organisation
Initial teacher-led discussion with whole class, followed by small group work and then a whole-class activity – a mock public inquiry. Another aspect of this lesson is the ongoing display about local issues in the form of a 'Newsboard', which has been built up from the beginning of the unit (see page 10).

What to do
(10 mins) Introduction
Introduce the lesson to the whole class by emphasising that the children will be discussing different viewpoints about places in the local area, then debating a proposed local development, and that mutual respect of different viewpoints is paramount.

Explain to the children the focus of the lesson:
● to express preferences for places in the local area, in terms of the features each has
● to be tolerant of and understand different viewpoints about the same land-use issue.

(1 hour 40 mins) Development
Part 1: small group activity (40 minutes)
● Ask the children, in groups, to sort photographs of places in the local area into those they 'like'

The local area

Vocabulary
Depends on
features of your
local area, but may
include:
environment
land-use
social
political
ecological
economic
sustainability

and 'dislike'. Then, focusing on those they dislike, children should list the features that caused this response (across the range of photographs). For example, depending on your local area, they might list features such as 'ugly buildings', 'dark woods' or 'busy roads'. The children should then sort their listed features into 'physical' and 'human'.

● Ask the children to explain why such features are less preferable than those in the places they 'liked', and to suggest solutions or improvements either through writing or drawing.

Part 2: whole-class activity (1 hour)

● As a class, choose a local land-use proposal or issue from those described on the 'Newsboard' display.

● Ask the children, in groups, to prepare for a 'public inquiry' into the issues surrounding the land-use proposal. Allocate roles to the children – each group should research the point of view of a particular character, such as a local businessman or woman, a local councillor, a parent of young children, an elderly person, a disabled person, or a school student. They should take into consideration the perspectives described in 'What you need and preparation', above, and think about how their character would feel about the new development. Each group should choose one person to represent their character and speak at the debate. If time permits, they could also prepare an appropriate costume for their character.

● Nominate two children: one as 'chair' and one as 'timekeeper', who should sit in the middle at the front of the class, facing the rest of the children. The 'character representatives' from each group should also come to the front, with those for the proposal on one side of the chair, and those against on the other side.

● The characters should take it in turns to talk about their views about the proposal. While each character is speaking, the other children should listen quietly. The chair should be in charge, asking each person to speak in turn, and making sure there are no arguments. Once all the characters have expressed their views, the other children can ask questions and give their ideas from the floor, one at a time.

● When the timekeeper says that time is up (after 20 minutes, perhaps), ask children to vote 'for' or 'against' the proposal, using a show of hands. They should try to be objective and vote according to the power of the persuasive arguments presented by the characters.

● After the vote, draw the session to a close by emphasising how people have different perspectives on issues, and the value of appreciating the views of others, even if they conflict with one's own.

Differentiation

All aspects of this activity are open-ended by outcome, as the opinions and contributions of each individual child are appreciated and valued by the others.

Assessing learning outcomes

Ephemeral evidence

● Contributions at the mock public inquiry.

Retainable evidence

● Accounts of those local features that the children dislike, and their proposed improvements.

Contrasting localities

Background information

Settlement function links what a place is like (its character) and where it is (its situation) to the main economic activity that goes on there (for example, industry, farming, tourism, and so on).

The notions of settlement size and settlement function are part of the concept of **settlement hierarchy**, which describes the relationship between different types of settlements: the number of people who live there, the work that can be done and jobs available, the services on offer including shopping and leisure facilities, and the role the settlement plays in administration. In this unit, children study one or more settlements of different sizes, and compare them with their own.

What is a city?

A city may be defined as a town made into a city by charter, usually the seat of a bishop. In studying cities and urban areas, children should be made aware of patterns of land-use and how this relates to economic activity. There may be identifiable zones within a city; for example, the Central Business District (CBD), manufacturing, industrial and residential areas (inner city and suburban). There may also be evidence of planning measures to restrict outward growth (green belt policy) and inner city redevelopment (regeneration of brownfield sites).

Green belt is the area of land around the edges of a city (or larger urban area), which is under strict planning control and is characteristically farm or recreational land. A brownfield site is an area where factories or old houses used to stand, which has since been cleared with a view to redevelopment. This regeneration process represents another measure to control outward growth.

What is a town?

A town may be defined as a populated area larger than a village, usually smaller than a city. There are different types of towns. For example, market towns are characteristically situated within good transport networks and are largely concerned with retail. Examples include Market Harborough and Appleby. There are also 'new towns', which represent a response to the pressures on the urban fringe of cities and larger urban areas. New towns are designed as self-contained urban centres and aim to relieve overcrowding, sometimes encouraging people to move to more remote (and possibly less desirable) areas. Examples of new towns include Warrington.

What is a village?

A village is traditionally defined as a large group of houses with a church. Key features usually include shops, a public house, a post office, a church, a community hall, houses, a school and possibly farms. Village settlements tend to be linear (in a line), nucleated (clustered) or dispersed (characteristic of farming villages). Some villages, where farming jobs have been reduced in number because of technological advancement in machinery, for example, and where good transport links exist, are populated by city commuters (some of whom may work from home using the Internet and other forms of communications technology).

It is essential when studying villages to look at services, buildings and building use, settlement shape, land-use, and economic activities/occupations.

What is a hamlet?

A hamlet is traditionally defined as a small group of houses, possibly with a church and often with some evidence of farming. This type of settlement is the smallest in the hierarchy, both in terms of population and area. Similar to villages, hamlets tend to be linear, nucleated or widely dispersed. Some may be dormant in terms of economic activity but can offer idyllic surroundings for residents (such as commuters, or retired workers). It is essential when studying hamlets to look at services (if any), buildings and building use, shape, economic activities and the wider geographical context, as there will be identifiable reasons why these settlements have never really grown.

UNIT: Contrasting localities

Enquiry questions	Teaching objectives	Teaching activities	Learning outcomes	Cross-curricular links
How does this city compare with our settlement? Where is this place and what is it like? Why is it like this?	• Ask geographical questions. • Analyse evidence and draw conclusions. • Use appropriate geographical vocabulary. • Use atlases, globes, maps and plans. • Use secondary sources of information. • Locate the places and environments studied. • Learn about a UK locality.	Children locate a contrasting city settlement on a globe and on world and regional maps. Study photographs through a transect of the city, from peripheral areas (possibly suburbs, green belt) to central areas (central business district etc). Children sequence the photographs and describe and explain patterns of land-use using photocopiable page 117. Children locate areas and features shown in the photographs on a small-scale street map. During discussion, children draw comparisons with their own settlement.	Children: • can match features (from photographs) to a map • develop an understanding of patterns of land-use in a city	
How does this town compare with our settlement? Where is this place and what is it like? Why is it like this?	• Ask geographical questions. • Collect and record evidence. • Analyse evidence and draw conclusions. • Use appropriate geographical vocabulary. • Use atlases, globes, maps and plans. • Use decision-making skills. • Identify how and why places change and how they may change in future. • Describe and explain how and why places are similar to and different from other places. • Learn about a UK locality. • Locate the places and environments studied.	Children locate a contrasting town settlement on a globe and world map (if possible) and on regional maps. Using an Ordnance Survey map, children record main routes into and out of the town on photocopiable page 118, and relate the growth/decline of the town to physical features, transport networks and other human activities. Children consider, in discussion, how and why their own settlement has changed over time.	• can use an Ordnance Survey map to identify routes and transport networks • begin to understand how transport networks may influence the growth and decline of towns	
How does this village compare with our settlement? Where is this place and what is it like? Why is it like this?	• Ask geographical questions. • Collect and record evidence. • Analyse evidence and draw conclusions. • Communicate in ways appropriate to the task and audience. • Use appropriate geographical vocabulary. • Use atlases, globes, maps and plans. • Use secondary information sources. • Use ICT to help in geographical investigations. • Learn about a UK locality. • Locate the places and environments studied.	Children locate a contrasting village settlement on regional maps. Using a map of the village, children note the shape of the settlement and its main features. Children then scan an aerial photograph into a computer software programme, and identify and colour-code main zones of land-use. They should relate features and land-uses to settlement function (eg farming, mining etc) In discussion, they compare their findings with the main features and land-uses of their own settlement.	• can use ICT to investigate land-use and to communicate findings. develop an understanding of the relationship between settlement shape, land-use and function	ICT: scanning, presenting and communicating findings
How does this hamlet compare with our settlement? Where is this place and what is it like? Why is it like this?	• Ask geographical questions. • Collect and record evidence. • Analyse evidence and draw conclusions. • Use appropriate geographical vocabulary. • Use atlases, globes, maps and plans. • Use secondary information sources. • Draw plans and maps. • Use decision-making skills. • Learn about a UK locality. • Identify how and why places change. • Describe and explain how and why places are similar to and different from other places. • Locate the places and environments studied.	Children locate a contrasting hamlet settlement on regional maps. Children study ground and aerial photographs and identify building types and surrounding land-uses. Photocopiable page 119 includes a variety of settlement features. Children use a base map of the hamlet being studied and consider what services would be needed for it to be developed into a village. Using secondary sources of evidence, children discuss and explain why this hamlet has never grown into a village. During discussion, the children draw comparisons with their own settlement.	• can use maps to plan for change • develop an understanding of factors that promote growth and decline in settlements.	

Resources
Globe; atlases; world and regional maps; Ordnance Survey maps showing city, town, village and hamlet to be studied; street map of city; sets of photographs of transect through city; aerial photographs of village; ground and aerial photographs of buildings in hamlet; 'Local Studies' software (*Mapping Skills* from Soft Teach Educational, ISBN 0 948 80817 9).

Display
Display to help children learn and remember new geographical vocabulary, eg urban, suburb, inner city, industrial, residential, manufacturing, green belt, urbanisation etc; display showing painting of route of transect through city, annotated with photographs, sketches and commentaries; display of transport links and features around the town in the form of a map painted by the children, annotated using OS symbols and a key, and showing commentaries explaining how the features contribute to the growth/decline of the settlement; display of children's computer-generated land-use maps of village; display of children's 'master plan' showing proposals for the development of the hamlet into a village.

How does this city compare with our settlement?

What you need and preparation

It is very helpful if children have carried out the activity described in 'What is our settlement like?' on page 14, and completed photocopiable page 115, before doing this lesson.

Using the following criteria, choose a city to be studied that contrasts with the children's own settlement. The contrasting city should ideally be:

- one that the children can visit as part of school life, on a residential visit or field trip for example
- one for which resources and photopacks such as those described below are readily available in school, or which is close enough for the class teacher to generate resources if necessary
- one with which the class teacher feels comfortable in terms of familiarity, subject knowledge and resources
- one that demonstrates clear contrasts with the children's own settlement.

You will need: a globe; world and regional maps including an Ordnance Survey map showing the contrasting city; aerial photographs of the city; ground photographs of sites along a transect through the city (one set for each group); copy of photocopiable page 117 for each child; copies of a street map of the city for each child to annotate; coloured pens; a copy of *Window* by Jeannie Baker (Red Fox, ISBN 0 099 18211 4) – this book of images represents the view from a window over a period of 24 years; it illustrates the process of urbanisation in a graphic and interesting way.

What to do

Introduction
15 mins

Introduce the lesson to the whole class by asking children to brainstorm what they think a city is and what they would expect to find in one. Ask the children to think of cities they have visited and the reasons why they went there. Introduce the city to be studied.

Explain to the children the focus of the lesson:

- to locate the position of the city to be studied on a map using four- or six-figure grid references
- to use ground photographs and maps to identify human and physical features and land-use at selected sites across the city being studied (along a transect)
- from this information, to describe and begin to explain how the land-use changes over the distance from the periphery to the centre and back out again
- to make comparisons with the children's own settlement.

Drawing on the children's expectations of cities, ask them to think about why a transect is a good strategy to use when exploring land-use in a large settlement. Show the children the ground photographs of the city being studied, and explain that each one was taken at a point along a transect through the city.

Using secondary sources (aerial and ground photographs, *Window* by Jeannie Baker), discuss the processes of urbanisation and introduce related processes such as green belt policy and regeneration of brownfield sites. Produce a display using words and photos to help children remember these new terms. Include the following terms, having discussed them with the children first: manufacturing, industrial, residential, inner city, urban, suburb. Discuss what is meant by 'physical (natural) features', 'human features' and 'land-use', and put these terms on the display.

Development
50 mins

Introduce the tasks: the children are going to study a certain city. First, ask the children to locate the city on a globe, if possible, and then on world, UK and regional maps. Ask them to locate the city, and particular features within the city, on an Ordnance Survey map, using four- or six-figure grid references.

**Contrasting
localities**

Divide the children into five groups of approximately six children. Using ground photographs of sites along the transect of the city, the children identify physical features, human features and land-uses (referring to the display of new geographical terms). Each group attempts to sequence the photographs, putting them in order along a line from the edges of the city to the centre. When they have put their photographs in the right order, the children use photocopiable page 117 to show the main land-uses across the city. (Children might find it helpful to have one or two examples of land-uses or features from the actual transect they are studying already written in on photocopiable page 117 to guide them in this activity.) They then attempt to explain why they are distributed in this way, and think about how the pattern compares with that in their own settlement (see 'What is our settlement like?' on page 14 and children's completed photocopiable page 115, if available). Once they have done this, the children should try to locate the areas and features shown in the photographs on a small-scale street map of the city, using a coloured pen to annotate.

10 mins Plenary

At the end of the lesson, the groups feed back the information they have found out about land-use patterns along the photographed transect. In so doing, children also consider how this compares to other cities they may have visited, and to their own settlement.

Differentiation

Less able children could be provided with a street map labelled with numbers corresponding to those on the photographs to help them locate and sequence the images. They could also be supplied with a word bank that includes labels to describe at least one feature or land-use in each photograph. If available, use human resources (classroom assistants and voluntary helpers) to work with Less able children.

More able children could use different sources to identify and describe similar or different land-use patterns in other cities.

Assessing learning outcomes

Ephemeral evidence

● Questions the children ask and the answers given to questions framed by the teacher during discussions and group work.
● Geographical vocabulary used by the children when undertaking the activity.
● Teamwork – how well do the children work together?

Retainable evidence

● Completed photocopiable page 117 – children identify patterns of land-use across the city, try to explain the pattern they find, and compare the main features and land-uses with those in their own settlement.

ICT opportunities
Children could twin with a school in the contrasting locality and exchange information by e-mail (using scanned image attachments).

Follow-up activities
● Practical fieldwork: children could observe, describe and record, through labelled field sketches and photography, features through or around their own settlement. Using these records, they could compare, contrast and analyse in more detail the differences and similarities in housing, land-use and leisure facilities between their own settlement and the contrasting city.
● Children could contribute to a class display, showing the transect route on a painted map of the city, annotated with photographs of features and written commentaries about the land-use in each sector.

(50 mins) How does this town compare with our settlement?

What you need and preparation

It is helpful if children have studied aspects and features of their own settlement before this lesson, for example through the activities described in 'Where are we?' and 'What is our local area like?' on pages 12 and 13.

Using the following criteria, choose a town to be studied that contrasts with the children's own settlement. The town should ideally be:
- one that the children can visit as part of school life, on a residential visit or field trip for example
- one for which resources are readily available in school, or which is close enough for the class teacher to generate resources if necessary
- one with which the class teacher feels comfortable in terms of familiarity, subject knowledge and resources
- one that demonstrates clear contrasts with the children's own settlement.

You will need: a globe; world and regional maps including Ordnance Survey maps showing the contrasting town; photocopiable page 118 (three copies for each child in the more able group, one copy each in the middle group, no copies for the less able group).

What to do

(10 mins) Introduction

Introduce the lesson to the whole class by asking children to brainstorm what they think a town is and what they would expect to find in one. Ask the children to think of towns they have visited and the reasons why they went there. Introduce the town to be studied.

Explain to the children the focus of the lesson:
- to locate the position of the town on maps
- to use Ordnance Survey maps to identify key features of the site and situation of town
- to use this information to explain why the town has grown, developed or declined
- to make comparisons with the children's own settlement.

Ask the children to brainstorm possible reasons for the growth and decline of settlements. For example, some farming villages have declined in terms of population over recent decades because machinery and technological advancements have reduced employment opportunities in manual work. Other places, for example Solihull (formerly a village), have expanded due to improved transport and proximity to larger settlements offering a wider range of employment opportunities. The children should then be encouraged to use this brainstormed list of reasons as a starting point for their task.

Discuss the concepts of the 'site' of a settlement (the physical profile of the land) and its 'situation' (where the settlement is in relation to other places).

(30 mins) Development

Using relevant Ordnance Survey 'Landranger' maps and UK atlases, children should consider what features of the site and situation of the town help to explain why it is like it is. For example, they should consider the shape of the land and other physical features, the transport links running through or close to the town, and the distances to other towns or important locations. The children should work in groups, as described under 'Differentiation' below.

Using photocopiable page 118, children draw a plan to record their ideas, and consider why this settlement is there. They are also asked to think about why the town is currently expanding or declining (delete the appropriate term on the photocopiable sheet, according to the town being studied).

Learning objectives
- Ask geographical questions.
- Collect and record evidence.
- Analyse evidence and draw conclusions.
- Use appropriate geographical vocabulary.
- Use atlases, globes, maps and plans.
- Use decision-making skills.
- Identify how and why places change and how they may change in the future.
- Describe and explain how and why places are similar to and different from other places.
- Learn about a UK locality.
- Locate the places and environments studied.

Lesson organisation

Initial teacher-led discussion with whole class, followed by ability-grouped enquiry activity. Children work in groups according to three ability levels, of up to six children; whole-class plenary session at end.

**Contrasting
localities**

Vocabulary
settlement
town
economic activity
market town
new town
manufacturing
industrial
residential
urban
suburbs
land-use
transport network

**ICT
opportunities**
Children could
produce a report
on the follow-up
fieldwork activity
using ICT.

**Follow-up
activities**
● Children could
observe, describe
and record
evidence of change
(growth and
decline) in their
own settlement,
using notes,
sketches,
photography, and
so on.
● Children could
contribute to a
class display,
showing the main
transport links and
other features on a
painted map of the
town, annotated
with Ordnance
Survey symbols
and written
commentaries
about the effects of
the various
features on the
growth or decline
of the settlement.

10 mins **Plenary**
At the end of the session, groups feed back the information they have found out about the town they have studied, and discuss their ideas about why the town has developed, grown or declined. They then consider the extent to which their own settlement has changed in terms of growth and decline.

Differentiation

It may be helpful to divide the class into three ability groups for this activity. Children of average ability could carry out the activity as described above.

More able children could be provided with several copies of photocopiable page 118, and could study the features of three or more contrasting towns (for example, a market town, a new town and a coastal town). They could consider how and why these different kinds of towns have developed.

Less able children could focus on the transport routes in to and out of a specified town, using an Ordnance Survey map. They could answer the following questions by writing or drawing (on separate paper, not on photocopiable page 118):
● How many roads come out of the town?
● Which towns do these roads lead to?
● How far is it to the nearest motorway?
● What jobs might people do in this town?

Add other questions appropriate to the town being studied; for example questions relating to other transport links, such as airports, railways, rivers or canals.

Assessing learning outcomes

Ephemeral evidence
● Questions the children ask and the answers given to questions framed by the teacher during discussions and group work.
● Geographical vocabulary used by the children when undertaking the activity.
● Identification of features of site and situation of settlement.
● Teamwork – how well do the children work together?

Retainable evidence
● Children's completed photocopiable page 118, or other accounts of their findings.

How does this village compare with our local area?

What you need and preparation

It is helpful if children have studied aspects and features of their own settlement before this lesson, for example through the activities described in 'Where are we?' and 'What is our local area like?' on pages 12 and 13.

Using the following criteria, choose a village to be studied that contrasts with the children's own settlement. The village should ideally be:

- one that the children can visit as part of school life, on a residential visit or field trip for example
- one for which resources are readily available in school, or which is close enough for the class teacher to generate resources if necessary
- one with which the class teacher feels comfortable in terms of familiarity, subject knowledge and resources
- one that demonstrates clear contrasts with the children's own settlement.

You will need: a globe; world and regional maps, including Ordnance Survey maps showing the village under study; aerial photographs and maps of village and of their own local area, for each group; access to a computer and scanner; 'Local Studies' software (*Mapping Skills* produced by Soft Teach Educational, ISBN 0 948 80817 9); *Paintbrush* (or other appropriate drawing software); display materials; blank acetates (two per group); acetate pens for each group.

What to do

Introduction
10 mins Introduce the lesson to the whole class by asking the children to list five things that they think they might find in a village, and to indicate whether they would find these features in a town or city. Ask the children to think of villages they know or have visited. Introduce the village to be studied.

Explain to the children the focus of the lesson:
- to locate the position of the village being studied on maps
- to use maps, aerial photographs and ICT to investigate the shape, features and main land-uses of the village settlement
- from this information, to relate features, land-uses and shape to the function of the settlement, and present the findings using ICT
- to make comparisons with the local settlement.

Remind children of the distinction between physical and human features. For example, rivers and relief (shape of the land) are physical features, as compared with residential and industrial areas, which are human features. Note examples of interaction between physical and human features, such as river pollution, or physical features of residential and industrial sites (hills, rivers and so on).

Demonstrate to the children how to scan an aerial photograph. It is worth asking the children to save this to the computer's hard disk rather than to floppy disk because of the large amount of memory necessary to store colour images. Most scanners are easy to use, but it may be worth producing a simple flow chart of instructions that is relevant to your scanner, as it will help children to remember the order in which each step should be taken. Explain that this will be the first stage of the activity, after which they will be working independently.

Briefly discuss how ICT will aid the manipulation and presentation of data, which will in turn inform their conclusions about the function of this village and how it compares with their own.

Development
1 hour 10 mins Ask each small group, while waiting for their turn to work on the computer, to use maps to

CHAPTER 1
UK LOCALITIES

Contrasting localities

Vocabulary
settlement
services
buildings
land-use
economic activities
occupation
village
nucleated
linear
dispersed

ICT opportunities
Children scan and process images using appropriate software.

Follow-up activities
● Using a printout from *Paintbrush* showing the main land-use zones in the village, children could devise a way of calculating land-use proportions using a transparent acetate overlay (for example, see photocopiable page 115).
● Using aerial photographs of their own settlement, children could repeat the activity and make direct comparisons with the village studied above, using the following headings as prompts:
● shape
● human features
● physical features
● land-use
● settlement function
● similarities and differences.

locate and identify the village settlement. (They could find the region on a globe or world map, and then focus in on the precise location using regional and Ordnance Survey maps.) The children should then place an acetate over a map or aerial view of the village being studied and define the general shape of the settlement using an acetate pen. They should then use different colours to denote the main human and physical features, such as landscape, water features, residential zones and so on.

Each group should then work independently on the computer on the following tasks. First, the children scan a vertical aerial photograph of the village settlement and save the image. Next, the children process land-use data from the photograph using *Paintbrush* (or other appropriate software). This involves opening the scanned image in the appropriate software program and denoting different land-uses using different coloured 'paints'. For example, they could paint over all residential areas shown on the scanned image using red paint. Similarly, blue could be used for water features. Children should save their processed image using a different filename, and print it off.

10 mins Plenary
When all groups have completed the task, and the children's work has been displayed, the groups feed back on their findings relating to the main features and land-uses of the village. In discussion, they compare these findings with the main features and land-uses of their own settlement.

Differentiation
Less able children could be involved in 'peer tutoring' by more able (ICT competent) children (there should be mixed-ability groups working at each computer).

More able children could use the 'Local Studies' mapping program to design their own village to accommodate workers employed by a new, large-scale, local industry.

Assessing learning outcomes
Ephemeral evidence
● Questions the children ask and the answers given to questions framed by the teacher during discussions and group work.
● Geographical vocabulary used by the children when undertaking the activity.
● Conclusions drawn about the shape and function of the village.
● The ICT skills used by the children when undertaking the activity.
● Teamwork – how well do the children work together?
Retainable evidence
● Computer-generated maps of land-use in the village.

**Contrasting
localities**

(1 hour) How does this hamlet compare with our local area?

What you need and preparation

It is helpful if children have studied aspects and features of their own settlement before this lesson, for example through the activities described in 'Where are we?' and 'What is our local area like?' on pages 12 and 13.

Using the following criteria, choose a hamlet to be studied that contrasts with the children's own settlement. The hamlet should ideally be:

- one that the children can visit as part of school life, on a residential visit or field trip for example
- one for which resources are readily available in school, or which is close enough for the class teacher to generate resources if necessary
- one with which the class teacher feels comfortable in terms of familiarity, subject knowledge and resources
- one that demonstrates clear contrasts with the children's own settlement.

You will need: a globe; world and regional maps, including Ordnance Survey maps showing the hamlet under study; ground and aerial photographs of the hamlet; base maps of the hamlet for each group, on which additional features can be marked; atlases; copy of photocopiable page 119 for each child (less able children only); scissors and glue.

What to do

(10 mins) Introduction

Introduce the lesson to the whole class by asking the children to quickly sketch three things they would expect to see in a hamlet. Ask the children to think of hamlets that they know or have visited. Introduce the hamlet being studied.

Explain to the children the focus of the lesson:

- to locate the position of the hamlet being studied using maps
- to use maps, aerial photographs and other secondary sources to investigate the shape, features and main land-uses of the hamlet settlement
- from this information, to consider additional features and the extent of growth necessary for this settlement to become a village
- to consider why this hamlet has never developed into a village or town
- to make comparisons with the children's own settlement.

Remind children of what they might find in a village and compare this with a town. Briefly revisit the concepts of 'site' (physical profile of the land) and 'situation' (where the settlement is located in relation to other places) with the children.

(40 mins) Development

The children identify the hamlet using maps at a range of scales. Then they use ground and aerial photographs to identify building types and surrounding land-uses. They consider which additional services would be needed for the hamlet to become a village. In groups, they should add features to a large base map of the hamlet being studied, to show how it could be developed into a village. (Less able children can cut out the shapes on photocopiable page 119 and stick them on to the base map, rather than writing or drawing their own annotations.)

Then, they should use secondary sources of information, including atlases, to discuss why this settlement has never grown into a village.

(10 mins) Plenary

When all groups have completed the activity, they should feed back on their findings using

Learning objectives
- Ask geographical questions.
- Collect and record evidence.
- Analyse evidence and draw conclusions.
- Use appropriate geographical vocabulary.
- Use atlases, globes, maps and plans.
- Use secondary sources of information.
- Draw plans and maps.
- Use decision-making skills.
- Learn about a UK locality.
- Identify how and why places change.
- Describe and explain how and why places are similar to and different from other places.
- Locate the places and environments studied.

Lesson organisation
Initial teacher-led discussion with the whole class, followed by small group activity (ability groupings); whole-class plenary discussion of base plans produced.

Vocabulary
settlement
hamlet
services
buildings
land-use
economic activities
occupation
village
nucleated
linear
dispersed

Follow-up activities
• The groups could exchange proposals for developing the settlement, and comment on each other's suggestions.
• As a class, or in broad ability groups, the children could arrive at a consensus on what features would best develop the hamlet, and produce a master plan for display to illustrate their final proposal.

their base plans as a visual aid. Use the following questions to frame the discussion:
● What features would you find in a village?
● What features have you added to your hamlet, and why?
● Why do you think this settlement has *not* developed in this way?
● What evidence supports your argument?
● What would need to happen here for this settlement to develop?
During the discussion, help the children to draw comparisons with their own settlement.

Differentiation
Less able children can use photocopiable page 119 to help them customise the map, showing how the hamlet could develop into a village.

More able children could refer to aerial views of villages, and written information about the services and main land-uses in villages, to help them see how the hamlet could develop.

Assessing learning outcomes
Ephemeral evidence
● Questions the children ask and the answers given to questions framed by the teacher during discussions and group work.
● The mapping skills used by the children when undertaking the activity.
● The choice of settlement features to develop the hamlet.
Retainable evidence
● Base map of hamlet being studied.

Economically Developing Countries

Introduction

In the National Curriculum (2000) for Geography, the Programme of Study for children at Key Stage 2, in its section on Breadth of Study, makes specific reference to the teaching of knowledge, skills and understanding through the study of two localities and three themes. One of the localities has to be in a less economically developed country (6b).

The following two units of work provide ideal opportunities, not only for studying localities in less economically developed countries, but also for integrating and investigating aspects of the three themes – 'water and its effects on landscapes and people...' (6c); 'how settlements differ and change...' (6d), and 'an environmental issue, caused by change in an environment...' (6e).

The four aspects of geography, as specified in the National Curriculum Programme of Study, can be taught through the study of a locality in a less economically developed country:

● **Geographical enquiry and skills** – for example, children identify and explain different views that people hold about topical geographical issues, such as the benefits and negative effects of the Aswan Dam in Egypt.

● **Knowledge and understanding of places** – for example, children explain why places are like they are in terms of weather conditions, local resources, and historical development.

● **Knowledge and understanding of patterns and processes** – for example, children recognise and explain patterns made by physical and human features in the environment, such as the pattern of human settlements along the Nile Valley.

● **Knowledge and understanding of environmental change and sustainable development** – for example, children recognise how decisions about places and environments, such as the building of the Aswan Dam, affect the future quality of people's lives.

The first unit in this chapter is on India and the second is on Egypt. In the QCA's *A Scheme of Work for Key Stages 1 and 2*, there is a unit on a locality in a less economically developed country. That is Unit 10, 'A village in India', which is designed for Year 4 children. The unit on India in this chapter is designed to build on, support, extend and supplement the QCA's unit on India.

As India is so large and diverse, it is felt that there is a need for children to develop a sound overview of the country before focusing on a village or town locality. This unit of work on India aims to help children gain access to the 'bigger' picture and to learn how different places are often interconnected.

Lessons are planned to develop locational knowledge through the use of secondary sources of information such as reference books, atlases, maps, photographs and the Internet. An understanding of the key question 'What is this place like?' is developed through an investigation of the climate of India (monsoon). Issues of sustainability are raised when comparisons of different forms of transport in rural and urban India are made, and this is further compared with transport in the UK.

The unit on Egypt may be used as an alternative to the study of India. Some of the generic ideas from QCA Unit 10, 'A village in India', can be adapted to use in a study of Egypt at Years 5 and 6. The unit on Egypt provides an ideal opportunity not only to study a locality in an economically less developed country (6b), but also to investigate two of the three themes listed above. This unit on modern Egypt could be linked with the National Curriculum for History (a world history study unit) – for example, with a study of the key features of a past society, such as Ancient Egypt (13).

The lessons in this unit of work are planned to develop locational knowledge, particularly of physical and human features of the River Nile. The importance of the River Nile to the economy of Egypt is present in every lesson. Issues of sustainability are investigated through a study of the positive benefits and negative effects of the Aswan Dam on the Nile Valley. The importance of the River Nile and tourism to the Egyptian economy is also examined. The hierarchy of settlements on the banks of the River Nile is investigated. The unit aims to help children to make sense of the world around them by contributing to their geographical knowledge, skills and understanding.

India – a land of many contrasts

Background information

India is a vast country of 3.3 million square kilometres (1.3 million square miles), with an estimated population of over 1 billion (2000). Much of India is a peninsula, which is surrounded by the Arabian Sea on the west and the Bay of Bengal on the east. India is a country of many contrasts: in its physical landscape and climate, from mountains with snow all year round to deserts; in its rich variety of lifestyles, customs and religions; and in the contrasts of its settlements, from the labour-intensive work in remote villages still lacking most of the developments of the last century, to the hustle and bustle of thriving cities, teeming with traffic and modern, high-tech industries. It is a country of great diversity – a country of enormous wealth, and also some of the worst poverty in the world.

India's climate is governed by the monsoon, the seasonal rain-bearing wind. Most of the country has three seasons: hot and dry (March to mid-June), monsoon or wet (June to late October) and cool and dry (October to March).

No single locality can reflect the huge diversity and richness of Indian life and culture, so to focus too sharply on the study of a village or city locality in India may lead to reinforcement of the children's misconceptions, and produce stereotypical images and prejudice. Life for children in India is as varied and different as it is for children in the UK. Children from rural, less-developed areas have very different lifestyles from children who live in urban areas, whether as members of rich families or as very poor children, some of whom live on the streets.

Modes of transport in India are many and varied. In rural areas, where the roads are unmade and there is great poverty, there are few motorised vehicles. But in the cities and towns the scene is very different. Most of the work on the land is still undertaken by hand and is very labour-intensive. Like all countries, India has to look to the future as it develops its transport networks. Sustainability and use of appropriate technology is an essential consideration as the population becomes more mobile.

The variety of Indian cooking is immense. It is colourful and aromatic; some of it is hot and spicy. Indian foods include Dhal, which is a crushed lentil soup; curries such as Rogan Josh (curried lamb), Bhujia (vegetable curry) and Dahi Maach (curried fish); Biriyani (chicken in orange-flavoured rice); Tandoori (meat marinated in herbs); Dhai (yoghurt to accompany curry); Samosa, Chapatis and Naan bread; Kulfi (Indian ice cream); Coconut Bafi (a sweet); and drinks such as Lasi (iced buttermilk), coconut milk and tea.

This unit of work aims to help children to obtain a balanced overview of India and to learn how different places are often interconnected. The unit hopes to help children to make sense of the world around them by contributing to their geographical knowledge, skills and understanding.

Resources

ActionAid resources on southern India:

- see www.chembakolli.com for a wide range of brand new resources on Chembakolli
- *Chembakolli: India village life* photopack £17.25
- *Take me to Chembakolli* CD-ROM £17.25
- *Footprints in the forest: a Chembakolli story* Big Book £17.25
- *Village life in India* CD-ROM £63.50
- *Working together: the people of Kanjikolly* video £28.75

(Prices accurate at time of publication.)

These, and other titles in the 'Village life' series, are available from: ActionAid Education, Chataway House, Leach Road, Chard TA20 1FR. Tel: 01460 238000, e-mail: deved@actionaid.org.uk, website: www.actionaid.org.

Material on Chembakolli appearing in this unit has been provided by ActionAid © 2000.

UNIT: India – a land of many contrasts

Enquiry questions	Teaching objectives	Teaching activities	Learning outcomes	Cross-curricular links
What is India like? Where is Asia? Where is India? Where are major landmarks, cities and physical features of India located? Which countries, seas and mountain ranges border India? What shape is India? How large is India in comparison with the UK? Why is India a land of many contrasts?	● Ask geographical questions. ● Collect and record evidence. ● Analyse evidence and draw conclusions. ● Use appropriate geographical vocabulary ● Use atlases, globes, maps and plans at a range of scales. ● Use secondary sources of information. ● Use ICT to help in geographical investigations. ● Locate the places and environments studied. ● Learn about a contrasting locality in an economically developing country. ● Recognise how places fit within a wider geographical context and are interdependent.	Using globes, world maps and atlases, children locate the positions of Britain, Europe, Asia, India, and other major features within India; Using atlases and maps of India, children locate and name the countries, seas and mountain ranges that border India, locate the positions of the main physical and human features of India and record this information on a blank map of India; Children copy and cut out maps of the UK and India at the same scale, compare relative sizes; Using all resources available, including the Internet, children find out some general information about India, and record it on photocopiable page 120. Children feed back to the class at the end what they have learned about India.	**Children:** ● are able to locate the positions of various countries, cities and physical features on globes and maps ● are able to locate the main physical and human features of India ● are able to use different methods of research to find ● out information are aware of the many contrasts in India	Literacy: reference skills. ICT: use the Internet as a source of information.
What is the climate like in India? What are the characteristics of the monsoon climate? How does this climate affect vegetation, agriculture, leisure activities, life and culture?	● Ask geographical questions. ● Analyse evidence and draw conclusions. ● Use appropriate geographical vocabulary. ● Use secondary sources of information. ● Use maps and plans at a range of scales. ● Identify and describe what places are like. ● Explain why places are like they are.	Children watch Programme 3 of *Coping with Climate* (BBC Education Video Plus) – 'Coping with the Wet'; Using information provided on photocopiable page 121, children write a weather report for Bangalore, and then plan what they would pack in a suitcase for a visit to Bangalore in early July. They consider what sorts of clothes etc to pack and why, and how their packing would be different for a visit in December; Children consider how the Indian monsoon climate is different from the climate in the UK.	● are able to interpret climatic data and use the information to produce a weather forecast ● are able to use information to prepare for a visit to India in the monsoon season	Citizenship: personal effectiveness.
What is life like for children in India?	● Ask geographical questions. ● Analyse evidence and draw conclusions. ● Use secondary sources of information. ● Use decision-making skills. ● Identify and describe what places are like. ● Locate the places and environments studied. ● Explain why places are like they are. ● Learn about a contrasting locality in an economically developing country.	Children brainstorm the things we need for a happy and healthy life. They discuss the differences between 'wants' and 'needs', and make lists under each of these headings (photocopiable page 122); In groups, children decide the six most important basic rights (needs) of all children; Teacher leads a discussion about the UN Convention on the Rights of the Child; Children consider the lives of some Indian children, as described on photocopiable page 123. They address the questions on photocopiable page 122, and consider whether the children described have their basic rights met.	● gain an understanding of what a place is like through the people who live there ● understand the differences between 'wants' and 'needs' (basic rights) ● gain an understanding of the UN Convention on the Rights of the Child. ● use all the information available to reflect on the lives of children in India	Health education: requirements for a healthy lifestyle. Citizenship: differences between wants and needs.
How do people travel in India? How do people travel about in the rural and urban areas of India? Why? What are the similarities and differences with modes of transport in the UK?	● Ask geographical questions. ● Analyse evidence and draw conclusions. ● Use appropriate geographical vocabulary. ● Use secondary sources of information. ● Use decision-making skills. ● Explain why places are like they are. ● Learn about a contrasting locality in an economically developing country.	Children use photographs of transport in India to help them describe the methods of transport. Using photocopiable page 124 to record their comments, they discuss: which methods of transport are used in rural areas and which in urban areas? What are the similarities with transport in rural and urban area in the UK? In groups, children discuss which fuel powers each type of transport and which is most environmentally friendly; They consider how transport in India might change in the future.	● develop an understanding of transport issues in different areas of India ● are able to compare the forms of transport they use with transport used in India ● develop an understanding of environmental and sustainability issues	Citizenship: use of different sources of fuel and transport.
What do people eat in India? What sort of food do the children eat? What utensils do they use to prepare food? How do they store the raw food? What do they use to eat the food with?	● Use appropriate geographical vocabulary. ● Use secondary sources of information. ● Identify and describe what places are like. ● Explain why places are like they are. ● Learn about a contrasting locality in an economically developing country. ● Use maps at a range of scales.	Children observe, touch, smell and taste a selection of raw foods and spices of the kind grown and used for cooking in India; School or class could hold an India theme day, and have an Indian banquet – make Indian dishes and have a tasting session; Children could dress in Indian clothes – invite an Indian lady or gentleman to show the children how the clothes are put on and worn; During the Indian banquet, play Indian music or invite Indian musicians into school to play traditional instruments; Children look at everyday artefacts from India. They discuss the artefacts and decide what they are used for, recording their ideas on photocopiable page 125.	● gain an insight into the lives of children in India through food, dance, music and artefacts ● learn skills to analyse and discuss artefacts from a basis of knowledge and understanding.	Literacy: instructional genre – recipes. RE: foods eaten and not eaten by different religious groups in India; Festivals.

Resources

Globes; world and regional maps of India; atlases; outline maps of the UK and India; photopacks eg *Chembakolli: India Village Life*, and *Bangalore: Indian City Life*, both produced by ActionAid, *India: Children's Needs, Children's Rights* (UNICEF); reference books; CD-ROMs eg *Village Life in India* (Cambridge University Press) and *Take me to Chembakolli* (ActionAid); *Coping with Climate* video and resource pack (BBC Education Video Plus); summaries of the UN Convention of the Rights of the Child; Indian clothes; raw foods and spices; ingredients for the Indian banquet dishes; ready-prepared Indian meals; CD or cassette of Indian music (for example, 'Putheri, songs of the adivasi' on *Take me to Chembakolli* CD-ROM or *Footprints in the forest clipart* CD from ActionAid, or *The music of India and Pakistan, the rough guide* from World Music Network); Indian musicians, dancers or storytellers (optional); artefacts hired from local Development Education Centre; access to the Internet; photocopiable pages 120–125

Display

Display of artefacts from everyday life in India; a selection of ingredients and spices of the kind grown in India; maps of India labelled with the regions from which the artefacts, ingredients and meals originate.

CHAPTER 2
ECONOMICALLY
DEVELOPING
COUNTRIES

India – a land
of many
contrasts

What is India like?

Learning objectives
- Ask geographical questions.
- Collect and record evidence.
- Analyse evidence and draw conclusions.
- Use appropriate geographical vocabulary.
- Use atlases, globes, maps and plans at a range of scales.
- Use secondary sources of information.
- Use ICT to help in geographical investigations.
- Locate the places and environments studied.
- Learn about a contrasting locality in an economically developing country.
- Describe and explain how and why places are similar to and different from other places.
- Recognise how places fit within a wider geographical context and are interdependent.

Lesson organisation
Teacher-led introduction, including brainstorm on what children know about India; in six groups of four to six, according to ability, children then locate places on globes and maps, and record them on blank maps of the world and India. Children investigate relative sizes of UK and India by cutting out maps at the same scale, then carry out research on India using various resources. Whole-class plenary session at the end.

Vocabulary
Britain
Europe
Equator
Tropics of Cancer and Capricorn
Asia
India
New Delhi
Calcutta
River Ganges
Himalayas
New Delhi
Western Ghats
Eastern Ghats
Bangalore
Mysore
Gudalur
Chembakolli

What you need and preparation
You will need: globes; world and regional maps of India; atlases; blank maps of the world and India for each group; outline maps for each child of the UK and India, at the same scale, to be cut out; photopacks eg *Chembakolli: India Village Life*, and *Bangalore: Indian City Life,* both produced by ActionAid; reference books; CD-ROMs such as *Village Life in India* (Cambridge University Press) and *Take me to Chembakolli* (ActionAid); access to the Internet (look at websites such as www.chembakolli.com, http://dir.yahoo.com/Regional/Countries/India/Country, http://comptonsv3.web.aol.com/); a copy of photocopiable page 120 for each child.

What to do

Introduction
10 mins
Introduce the lesson to the whole class by brainstorming with the children what they already know about India and where it is located in the world.

Explain to the children the focus of the lesson:
- to use atlases, globes and maps to locate India, within the context of the world and in relation to the UK
- to use atlases and maps to find some of India's human and physical features
- to use secondary sources of information, including the Internet, to find out about India.

Development
55 mins
Using atlases and maps of India at a range of scales, children should work in six groups of four to six according to ability, and locate the following places and features, recording them on a blank map of the world: United Kingdom, Europe, Equator, Tropics of Cancer and Capricorn, Asia, India, New Delhi, Calcutta, River Ganges, Himalayas, New Delhi, Western Ghats, Eastern Ghats, Bangalore, Mysore, Gudalur, Chembakolli.

The children should also locate and name the countries, seas and mountain ranges that border India, and mark these on their maps.

To gain some understanding of the relative size of India compared to the UK, the children should cut out maps of the UK and India (at the same scale), and then see how many times the UK will fit into India.

Each group should now carry out research to find general information about India using resources such as atlases, photopacks, reference books, CD-ROMs, the Internet and so on. They should use photocopiable page 120 to guide their research and to record their findings.

Plenary
10 mins
At the end of the session, groups should feed back information they have found out about India and reflect on the ease of use of the different sources of information. In doing so, children should consider the nature of the information and how up-to-date that information is.

Differentiation
Less able children should not be given photocopiable page 120. Instead, direct them to use a simple reference book and particular websites on the Internet to find out about India, such as:

CHAPTER 2
ECONOMICALLY
DEVELOPING
COUNTRIES

India – a land
of many
contrasts

population and size, national flag, source and length of two major Indian rivers, names of four major cities and where they are, how the weather changes over the year, types of industry.

More able children should use reference books and the Internet to find additional information about India that they find interesting, over and above the items listed on photocopiable page 120, and feed this back to the other children at the end.

Assessing learning outcomes

Ephemeral evidence

- Observation of, and discussion with, the children as they carry out the activities.
- Questions the children ask and the answers given to questions framed by the teacher.
- Geographical vocabulary used by the children when undertaking the activity.
- Information selected by the children and their critical use of this information.
- Children's reflection on the value of the different sources of information.
- Teamwork – how well do the children work together?

Retainable evidence

- Children's completed photocopiable page 120 and other records.

ICT opportunities
Use of the Internet and CD-ROMs plays an integral part in this lesson.

Follow-up activity
Children could make their own 'ABC of India', or zig-zag book.

What is the climate like in India?
(1 hour 15 mins)

What you need and preparation

You will need: Programme 3 of *Coping with Climate* (BBC Education Video Plus) – 'Coping with the Wet'; OHT of worksheet 8 from *Coping with Climate Resource Pack* – 'The burst of the monsoon'; copy of photocopiable page 121 for each child; OHP.

What to do

Introduction *(10 mins)*

Explain to the children the focus of the lesson:
- to find out what they know about the climate and weather in India
- to develop the correct geographical vocabulary and terms to describe features of India's climate
- to develop an understanding of how the weather and climate of a place has a direct impact on the way of life of the people who live there – their homes, clothes, agriculture and so on.
- to explain in particular why India is like it is and how the monsoon climate affects every facet of life there.

Before starting the lesson, find out what the children already know about the Indian climate. Introduce a simple baseline assessment by asking each child to write down briefly what they think the weather is like in India and why. Children should then feed back their ideas to the others.

Discuss with the class the differences between climate and weather.

Development *(1 hour)*

As a class, watch Programme 3 of *Coping with Climate* (BBC Video Plus) – 'Coping with the Wet'. After the programme, ask the children to look at an OHT of worksheet 8 from the *Coping with Climate Resource Pack*, entitled 'The burst of the monsoon'. Discuss the progress of the monsoon from mid-June, and label on the OHT the dates when the monsoon arrives in certain places in India. Look at the climatic data for

Learning objectives
- Ask geographical questions.
- Analyse evidence and draw conclusions.
- Communicate in ways appropriate to the task and audience.
- Use appropriate geographical vocabulary.
- Use secondary sources of information.
- Use maps and plans at a range of scales.
- Use ICT to help in geographical investigations.
- Identify and describe what places are like.
- Explain why places are like they are.
- Learn about a contrasting locality in an economically developing country.

Lesson organisation
Initial teacher introduction and simple assessment activities; the children watch a video on the monsoon climate, and discuss afterwards what they have learned as a class. Individual work on the activities on photocopiable page 121: writing a weather report, packing a suitcase for a visit to an Indian city. Whole-class plenary session at end – general discussion on the main features of the monsoon climate and how this climate is different from that in the UK.

CHAPTER 2
ECONOMICALLY DEVELOPING COUNTRIES

India – a land of many contrasts

Vocabulary
monsoon
torrential rain
humid
rainfall
tropical
equator
annual
temperature
flooding

ICT opportunities
Children could use the Internet to find current weather information, and use spreadsheet and graph packages to display climatic data.

Follow-up activity
Children could work in groups to prepare a television documentary on how the climate affects the lives of people who live there. They could use interviews with 'experts', maps, photographs and paintings in their programme, and present it to the rest of the class.

Bangalore, provided on photocopiable page 121, and discuss what the children notice.

Ask the children to pretend they are reporters for the *Indian Daily Star*, a national newspaper. Ask each child, working individually, to write a weather report for Bangalore for July 10th, using the data on photocopiable page 121. The children should include a map in their report and an interview with a local rice farmer – how does the rice farmer feel when the monsoon arrives?

Ask the children to imagine they are going to visit a friend in Bangalore in early July. What sorts of clothes and so on should they pack and why? If they visited their friend in December, how would their packing be different?

5 mins **Plenary**
At the end of the lesson, there should be a whole-class discussion to recap on the main features of the monsoon climate and how this climate is different from that in the UK.

Differentiation
Less able children could be provided with a writing frame to support their written weather report. They could draw the items they would pack for their visit to Bangalore, rather than describing them in words. Use human resources (classroom assistants/voluntary helpers), if available, to work with less able children.

More able children could compare and contrast the monsoon climate with the climate in the UK and illustrate to younger children (in Year 4, say) what the monsoon climate is like. If it can be arranged, the children could actually explain the Indian monsoon climate to Year 4 children, and discuss with them how this type of climate affects the people who live in India.

Assessing learning outcomes
Ephemeral evidence
● Observation of, and listening to, the children as they write their weather reports and complete the suitcase activity.
● Geographical vocabulary used by the children when undertaking the activity.
Retainable evidence
● Each child's initial knowledge of the climate of India (baseline assessment activity).
● Each child's weather report.
● Each child's suitcase activity.

1 hour 15 mins What is life like for children in India?

Learning objectives
● Ask geographical questions.
● Analyse evidence and draw conclusions.
● Use secondary sources of information.
● Use decision-making skills.
● Identify and describe what places are like.
● Locate the places and environments studied.
● Explain why places are like they are.
● Learn about a contrasting locality in an economically developing country.

What you need and preparation
You will need: written summaries of the UN Convention on the Rights of the Child, worded as appropriate for the children's abilities (to be found in *Talking Rights, Taking responsibility* (UNICEF, 1998); photographs of environments similar to those described on photocopiable page 123, from *Chembakolli: Indian Village Life* and *Bangalore: Indian City Life* (photopacks produced by ActionAid); a copy of photocopiable page 122 for each child; a copy of photocopiable page 123 for each group; *I Is for India* by P Das (Frances Lincoln, ISBN 0 711 21056 X) for general reference.

What to do
15 mins **Introduction**
Brainstorm with the whole class what they feel is necessary for them to live a happy and healthy life. Discuss the children's views.

CHAPTER 2
ECONOMICALLY
DEVELOPING
COUNTRIES

India – a land
of many
contrasts

Explain to the children the focus of the lesson:

- to learn the differences between 'wants' and 'needs'
- to learn about 'basic rights' and the UN Convention on the Rights of the Child
- to learn about the lives of children in India, and consider whether their basic needs are being met.

As a class, the children discuss the differences between 'wants' and 'needs'. Then, in mixed-ability groups of four to six, the children list the things that fit under each of these headings, from the first part of photocopiable page 122.

As a class, discuss whether 'wants' and 'needs' differ for different people. Would they be the same for children in India as for themselves, for example? What reasons do the children have for their answers?

45 mins Development

In the same mixed-ability groups of four to six, children discuss and reflect on the content of their 'needs' column on photocopiable page 122. As a group, the children decide on the six most important basic rights for all children. Then, as a whole class, discuss each group's list and see if the children can come up with a set of six needs that the whole class agrees upon.

Give each group a summary of the UN Convention of the Rights of the Child (differentiated for the ability of the children). Ask them to discuss the Articles of the Convention and to decide whether they agree or disagree with them.

Give each group a copy of photocopiable page 123 and photographs from *Chembakolli: Indian Village Life* and *Bangalore: Indian City Life* (photopacks produced by ActionAid). Children should read the brief descriptions of the lives of Madhan, Badichi, Penchi, Babu, and Khushboo, who have a variety of different backgrounds and lifestyles. (Children may hold misconceptions about the lives of Indian children – that they are all very poor, for example – and should be encouraged to see that there is as much variety amongst Indian children as there is amongst children in the UK.) After reading the descriptions, the children should look at the photographs, which show the kinds of environments in which the children live, and then answer the questions on the second part of photocopiable page 122. Finally, in their groups, the children should decide whether they think each child's basic needs are being met.

15 mins Plenary

As a class, the children should recap on their discussions about whether or not the basic needs of each of the named children from India described on photocopiable page 123 are being met.

Differentiation

This lesson is accessible to children of all abilities. The work is undertaken in mixed-ability groups. Less able children may benefit from working with human resources (classroom assistants/voluntary helpers), if available.

More able children could read Articles 31 and 32 of the UN Convention on the Rights of the Child:

Article 31 says that children have the right to rest, leisure and play.

Article 32 says that children have the right to be protected from working in places or conditions that are likely to damage their health or get in the way of their education. If someone is making money out of their work, they should be paid fairly.

In groups, children could discuss these Articles. Does the group think the five Indian children are having their basic needs met, in accordance with the Articles of the Convention? If not, how are their rights being denied?

**CHAPTER 2
ECONOMICALLY
DEVELOPING
COUNTRIES**

India – a land
of many
contrasts

Assessing learning outcomes
Ephemeral evidence
● Observation of, and listening to, the children as they discuss 'wants' and 'needs', basic rights and the lifestyles of the Indian children.
● Geographical vocabulary used by the children when undertaking the activity.
Retainable evidence
● Group responses to questions on photocopiable page 122.

① How do people travel in India?
1 hour

Learning objectives
● Ask geographical questions.
● Analyse evidence and draw conclusions.
● Use appropriate geographical vocabulary.
● Use secondary sources of information.
● Use decision-making skills.
● Explain why places are like they are.
● Learn about a contrasting locality in an economically developing country.

Lesson organisation
Initial introduction to find out what children know about transport in the UK. In mixed-ability groups, children discuss methods of transport in rural and urban areas in India and the UK, and complete the table on photocopiable page 124. They review the fuel used and its sustainability, and consider questions on photocopiable page 124. Whole-class plenary session to reflect on the pros and cons of different modes of transport in India.

What you need and preparation
You will need: photographs of transport in India, from the website www.chembakolli.com, from photopacks such as *Chembakolli: Indian Village Life* and *Bangalore: Indian City Life* (ActionAid), or from *India: Children's Needs, Children's Rights* (UNICEF); a copy of photocopiable page 124 for each child.

What to do
(10 mins) Introduction
Find out what the children already know about transport in the UK. In mixed-ability groups, ask the children to write down briefly what sorts of transport are available in the UK, and then to highlight the modes of transport they use most frequently. Then ask the children to write down what kinds of journeys they make in each of the highlighted modes of transport.
Explain to the children the focus of the lesson:
● to learn about the methods of transport in India
● to compare and contrast transport used in India with transport in the UK
● to develop the correct geographical vocabulary to describe transport in India
● to develop an understanding of sustainability in transport.

(40 mins) Development
In mixed-ability groups, ask the children to look at photographs from the Chembakolli and Bangalore, and other photographs of transport in India. They should discuss the methods of transport being used, and where they are being used (in rural or urban areas). Children record this information using the table on photocopiable page 124.
Children then discuss transport in the UK, and decide if and where each form of transport described in the table is used in the UK. They each record this information in the same table on photocopiable page 124, and then discuss the similarities and differences between transport in India and transport in the UK.
In the same mixed-ability groups, children discuss the questions on photocopiable page 124, and record their responses on the page. Provide copies of photocopiable page 123 from the previous lesson to remind children about Madhan, Badichi, Penchi, Babu and Khushboo.

(10 mins) Plenary
At the end of the lesson, conduct a general class discussion about the advantages, disadvantages and any problems associated with the different modes of transport used in

India – a land
of many
contrasts

India. Ask the children to predict how they think transport in India will change over the next ten years.

Differentiation
This lesson is accessible to children of all abilities. All the work is undertaken in mixed-ability groups. Use human resources (classroom assistants/voluntary helpers), if available, to work with less able children.

Assessing learning outcomes
Ephemeral evidence
- Observation of, and listening to, the children as they discuss the photographic evidence
- Children's use of critical thinking skills.
- Geographical vocabulary used by the children when undertaking the activity.
- Teamwork and co-operation – how well do the children work together in groups?

Retainable evidence
- Each group's initial work on modes of transport in the UK, produced during the introduction to the lesson.
- Each child's completed photocopiable page 124.

> **Vocabulary**
> transport
> sustainability
> pedal-powered
> rickshaw
> motorised rickshaw
> cart pulled by oxen
> horse or camel

> **ICT opportunities**
> Children could use the Internet to access information about transport and transport issues in India.

> **Follow-up activity**
> Extreme overcrowding and pollution are becoming major problems in Indian cities. Children could conduct some research (using reference books, the Internet and so on) to find out about these problems, their causes and some of the solutions to the problems. Ask the children to write a short passage, describing what they would hear, see and smell on a busy street in Bangalore.

3-4 hours What do people eat in India?

What you need and preparation
The variety of Indian cooking is immense. It is colourful and aromatic; some of it is hot and spicy (see 'Background information' on page 30). Recipes to prepare Indian dishes are easily available and many are easy for children to make and taste. Remember that the food and banquet require shopping time, preparation time and supervised access to a cooking area for the children. Authentic, ready-prepared Indian meals are also available for use in tasting sessions.

Indian musicians and dancers may be available in your area. Contact your local Development Education Centre (DEC) for details. Also, the DEC is often a source of genuine artefacts, which may be borrowed on a loan system for the third part of this lesson.

You will need: Indian clothes for the children to wear (prepared by parents and helpers from the Indian community, if possible); raw foods and spices of the kind grown and used in India; ingredients for the dishes to be served at the Indian banquet (plus preparation and cooking time in a suitable cooking area); ready-prepared Indian meals; CD or cassette of Indian music (for example, 'Putheri, Songs of the Adivasi' on *Take me to Chembakolli* CD-ROM, *Footprints in the Forest Clipart* CD from ActionAid, or *The Music of India and Pakistan, the Rough Guide* from World Music Network); Indian musicians, dancers or storytellers (optional); genuine everyday artefacts hired from local Development Education Centre (enough for three per group); three copies of photocopiable page 125 for each group (one copy for each artefact).

> **Learning objectives**
> - Use appropriate geographical vocabulary.
> - Use secondary sources of information.
> - Identify and describe what places are like.
> - Explain why places are like they are.
> - Learn about a contrasting locality in an economically developing country.
> - Use maps at a range of scales.
>
> **Lesson organisation**
> This lesson requires time in advance to prepare clothes, food and cooking. Organisation of the Indian theme day itself can vary as required, but may include children touching, smelling, tasting and feeling Indian foods and ingredients; dressing in Indian dress; music, dance and storytelling; and looking at everyday artefacts from India. Children record ideas about the artefacts on photocopiable page 125. Children work, when appropriate, individually, in mixed-ability groups or as a whole class.

CHAPTER 2
ECONOMICALLY
DEVELOPING
COUNTRIES

**India – a land
of many
contrasts**

Vocabulary
dhal
curries
rogan josh
bhujia
dahi maach
biriyani
tandoori
dhai
samosa
chapatis
naan bread
kulfi
coconut bafi
lasi
coconut milk
tea aromatic
artefact

What to do

Introduction

As a class, ask the children to discuss the following questions:

- What sort of food do the children eat at home?
- What utensils do they use to prepare the food with?
- How do they store the raw ingredients?
- What do they use to eat the food with?
- What kinds of music do they listen to, and why?
- What kinds of dancing do they do?
- How do all these things reflect the children's country, culture and way of life?
  Explain to the children the focus of the lesson:
- to learn about what different parts of India are like through dance, music, food and artefacts
- to learn about the way of life in different parts of India
- to use these experiences to help explain why India is like it is
- to study maps of India.

Development

Part 1: Food and banquet (1 hour)

Display a selection of raw ingredients and spices that are grown in India and used for cooking. Encourage the children to look at, touch, smell and taste them. Display a map of India, labelled with the region from which each ingredient comes. Discuss with the children what each food is, and where it is used.

Then children can taste cooked dishes from different parts of India and discuss them in mixed-ability groups. Again, show a map of India, labelled with the region from which each dish comes. During this Indian banquet, ask the children to dress in Indian clothes. If possible, ask a member of the local Indian community to show the children how the clothes are put on and worn. Play Indian music (see suggested sources under 'What you need and preparation').

At the end, discuss with the children what they liked and did not like about the dishes and the music. What did they think about the clothes?

Part 2: Music and dance (1 hour)

If possible, invite Indian musicians and dancers in to school to demonstrate traditional instruments and dances. Otherwise, the length of this session can be reduced, and Indian music played from a CD during the banquet.

Part 3: Investigating Indian artefacts (1 hour)

The children should work in mixed-ability groups of four to six, depending on the size of the class. Display a selection of artefacts used in India on each table (approximately three artefacts to a table – these can be passed around if you do not have many artefacts). If appropriate, place a map of India on the table, labelled with the region from which each artefact comes. Explain to the children that these are everyday articles used by children and adults in India. Encourage the children to look at, touch and smell them.

Explain to the children, as a class, that around the world artefacts are made for different purposes and needs by different societies, from different materials and with different and appropriate technologies. Give each group a copy of photocopiable page 125 for each artefact they look at. You could use a typical western artefact, such as a teabag, and go through the table showing the children what they should look at and how to answer the questions.

Ask each group to look at and discuss each of the Indian artefacts on their table, and to complete one copy of photocopiable page 125 for each artefact. Can the children name the artefact?

CHAPTER 2
ECONOMICALLY
DEVELOPING
COUNTRIES

India – a land
of many
contrasts

When all the groups have finished, conduct a class discussion about the different artefacts and how they may be used.

15 mins **Plenary**
At the end of the whole lesson, bring the class together and discuss what the children have learned about life in parts of India from the foods, music and artefacts they have experienced, that they didn't know before.

Differentiation
This lesson is accessible to children of all abilities. All the work is undertaken in mixed ability groups. Use human resources (classroom assistants/voluntary helpers), if available, to work with less able children.

Assessing learning outcomes
Ephemeral evidence
● Observation of, and listening to, the children's discussion while they are preparing and taking part in the banquet and looking at the artefacts.
● Children's use of critical thinking skills.
● The geographical vocabulary used by the children when undertaking the activities.
● Teamwork and co-operation – how well do the children work together in the groups?
Retainable evidence
● Each group's completed photocopiable page 125 for each artefact studied.

ICT opportunities
Children could use the Internet to find additional information about food, music and dance in India.

Follow-up activity
In pairs, the children could decide upon, and list, eight items that they use regularly, which would represent their lives to children in India. Then, in mixed-ability groups of three sets of pairs, children could share each other's lists and try to negotiate eight items that the group as a whole feel represent their lives. The children can discuss how difficult it is to represent themselves with just a few objects.

Egypt – a land of surprises

Background information

Egypt is a country of over 1 million square kilometres (386 559 square miles; four times the size of the UK), and has a population of about 62.5 million people – nearly half live in cities. Cairo, the capital, is the largest city in Africa and is the most densely populated. Most of the land in Egypt (97%) is desert, receiving very little rainfall; the remaining 3% being the narrow strips of rich, fertile land on either side of the River Nile and its delta.

The River Nile is 6670 kilometres long, and has two main tributaries, the White Nile and the Blue Nile. It flows from south to north, through Uganda, Sudan and Egypt. Its source is said to be in the mountains near Lake Victoria, from where it flows, over waterfalls, to lower ground. From there, the river winds its way through the Sahara desert, becoming increasingly sluggish and fanning out into a delta before it flows into the Mediterranean Sea.

For the Egyptians, life without the River Nile would be almost impossible. Over the years, the Egyptians have found different ways of controlling the river, not only for agriculture but also to produce power (hydroelectric power from the Aswan Dam) and for transport and trade.

The Aswan Dam was built in 1960 and opened in 1971. It provides hydroelectric power for the whole of Egypt and controls the flooding of the Nile, while also providing irrigation for farmers, so two or three crops can be grown each year. The dam, which is 11 metres high and made of packed sand, gravel and rubble, also created Lake Nasser, the largest artificial lake in the world (500 kilometres long), which provides a place for recreation and wildlife. There are 180 water gates, and the crest of the dam is 3830 metres along its length. It took 50 000 people to build it. The Aswan Dam is the largest dam in the world and Lake Nasser is so big that the surface area of water has affected the region's climate. There is now a growing concern that the building of the dam and the creation of the artificial lake could be creating more environmental problems than it has solved.

Most of the people who live in rural areas make their living from farming, but in spite of this Egypt has to import two-thirds of its grain, mainly from the USA. Egypt exports cotton, oranges, rice, potatoes and oil. The country also earns a lot of money from tourism; the tourist trade is very important to the modern Egyptian economy. Many tourists flock to the Nile and its immediate surrounding area because of Egypt's rich historical legacy. People have been farming in the valley of the River Nile for at least 7000 years. The pyramids at Giza are considered one of the Seven Wonders of the World. The magnificent architecture and temples of Luxor make it one of Egypt's greatest tourist destinations. Feluccas and old barges shuffle between luxury cruise ships on the River Nile.

The final lesson plan in this unit looks at a village (el Beled – which is based on villages in Upper Egypt near Qena), a town (Quesna) and a city (Cairo). This provides a cross-section of settlement types and thus helps to avoid children gaining a very stereotypical image of life in Egypt.

UNIT: Egypt – a land of surprises

Enquiry questions	Teaching objectives	Teaching activities	Learning outcomes	Cross-curricular links
Where is the River Nile? How many countries does the River Nile flow through? Which way is the river flowing? What happens when it reaches the sea?	• Ask geographical questions. • Use appropriate geographical vocabulary. • Use atlases, globes, maps and plans at a range of scales. • Use secondary sources of information. • Locate the places and environments studied. • Describe where places are. • Learn about a contrasting locality in an economically developing country.	Using globes, world maps and atlases, children locate the positions of Britain, Europe, the Equator, the Tropics of Cancer and Capricorn, Africa, Egypt, River Nile, Quesna, Cairo and Luxor. Children watch the BBC *Landmarks* video, *The Gift of the Nile*, and discuss how the Nile affects the lives of the Egyptian people. Children look at the River Nile on a map. On photocopiable page 126, they identify and label various features of the Nile from source to sea.	Children: • are able to use maps at a variety of scales to access information, interpret it and use it appropriately. • begin to understand the importance of the River Nile to Egyptians.	Numeracy: measurement, scale.
How do the Egyptians control the River Nile? Why is the River Nile so important to Egypt? Where is the Aswan Dam located? Why was it built? What impact did it have on the lives of the Egyptians (eg on their farming methods)?	• Use ICT to help in geographical investigations. • Collect and record evidence. • Analyse evidence and draw conclusions. • Investigate water and its effects on landscapes and people. • Identify and explain different views that people, including themselves, hold about topical geographical issues. • Recognise how and why people may seek to create and manage sustainable environments. • Communicate in ways appropriate to the task and audience.	Children watch the relevant parts of the BBC *Landmarks* video, *The Gift of the Nile*, and use photographs from *The Thread of the Nile* photopack, reference books and the Internet to find out about the importance of the River Nile to the Egyptians. Children role-play a debate on the positive benefits and negative effects of the Aswan Dam and its impact on the way the Nile is used (photocopiable page 127). Using a discussion genre writing frame (photocopiable page 128), children write a newspaper report on the debate for the *Egyptian Daily News*.	• understand the importance of the River Nile to Egyptians. • realise that the river is central to the whole economy and well-being of the country. • understand that all developments have impacts on the environment – some good, some less so. are able to discuss the positive benefits and negative effects of the Aswan Dam.	ICT: use of the Internet for reference work. Literacy: discussion work.
Why is the River Nile important for tourism? What images of the Nile predominate in the tourist brochures? What sort of images are missing? What do tourists need on board a cruise ship? What do cruise passengers require from the places they stop at?	• Ask geographical questions. • Use appropriate geographical vocabulary. • Use secondary sources of information. • Use ICT to help in geographical investigations. • Use decision-making skills. • Identify and explain different views that people, including themselves, hold about topical geographical issues. • Communicate in ways appropriate to the task and audience. • Investigate water and its effects on landscapes and people. • Learn about a contrasting locality in an economically developing country.	Children collect tourist brochures and adverts about holidays in Egypt and cruises on the Nile. They analyse the genre of writing. Children imagine they are on the Board of Directors of a holiday company that owns a Nile cruise ship. The Directors have to discuss items on a meeting agenda: on-board entertainment, on-shore excursions, items the cruise ship requires from stops in port. Children discuss the agenda items, in role, and make decisions and action points. Children design a cruise itinerary with eight activities for passengers (photocopiable page 129). Children produce a tourist brochure or a class display.	• are able to criticise and evaluate tourist information. • are able to use all available information and make reasoned decisions. • are able to understand the importance of the River Nile to the tourist industry in Egypt and also the importance of the tourist trade to the economy of the country.	Literacy: persuasive genre of writing. Citizenship: eco-tourism. History: Ancient Egypt.
What kinds of settlements are on the banks of the Nile?	• Ask geographical questions. • Identify and describe what places are like. • Study maps at a range of scales. • Locate the places and environments studied. • Describe and explain how and why places are similar to and different from other places. • Recognise how places fit within the wider geographical context and are interdependent. • Investigate how settlements differ and change, including why they differ in size and character.	Class decides on an Egyptian village, town and city to investigate eg el Beled (village in upper Egypt near Qena), el Quesna (market town in the delta) and Cairo (a city). Class is divided into three mixed-ability research groups. One group investigates a village, another looks at a town, and the third studies a city. Using all available resources (photographs, photopacks, video evidence, reference books, Internet etc), each child undertakes a settlement survey, and each group creates a 'fact file' for their settlement (photocopiable page 130). Using their fact file, each group prepares and presents its information in the form of a documentary programme for children's TV, with interviews, reports and tourist information, etc. The age of the intended audience is 8 to 11.	• are able to investigate how settlements in Egypt differ and change, including why they differ in size and character. • are able to use a variety of secondary sources of evidence to identify and describe what places are like and how they are similar and different from other settlements.	History: Ancient Egypt. Literacy: informational texts, speaking and listening

Resources

Globes; world maps and atlases; maps of Africa and Egypt (different scales); reference books; photographs; *The Thread of the Nile* photopack (TIDE, Development Education Centre, Birmingham (1996) ISBN 0 948 83846 9); *Cairo – Four children and their city*, photopack (Oxfam); BBC *Landmarks* video (programmes entitled *The Gift of the Nile* and *Life in Cairo*; *The Day of Ahmed's Secret*, by F Parry; *Ancient Lands* CD-ROM (Microsoft); tourist brochures that include visits to Egypt and cruises on the River Nile; highlighter pens; display materials; access to computers with word-processing or DTP software; access to Internet; photocopiable pages 126–130 (photocopiable page 127 copied onto card and cut out, photocopiable page 130 copied in two parts, enlarged).

Display

Class display showing ideas for activities on a cruise down the River Nile, or class brochure for such a holiday.

CHAPTER 2
ECONOMICALLY DEVELOPING COUNTRIES

Egypt – a land
of surprises

① Where is the River Nile?
(1 hour)

Learning objectives
- Ask geographical questions.
- Use appropriate geographical vocabulary.
- Investigate water and its effects on landscapes and people.
- Use atlases, globes, maps and plans at a range of scales.
- Use secondary sources of information.
- Locate the places and environments studied.
- Describe where places are.
- Learn about a contrasting locality in an economically developing country.

Lesson organisation
Whole-class teacher-led introduction to the River Nile; children work in pairs to locate the River Nile on maps, then the class watch a video on Egypt. Children work individually, labelling a map of the Nile from source to mouth using reference books and photocopiable page 126. Whole-class plenary session at the end.

Vocabulary
mouth
source
tributaries
delta
Aswan Dam
Lake Nasser
reservoir
estuary
desert
flow
flooding
drought
erosion
deposition

What you need and preparation
You will need: globes; atlases; maps of Africa and Egypt at different scales; information books about the Nile; BBC *Landmarks* video on Egypt (the programme entitled 'Gift of the Nile'); a copy of photocopiable page 126 for each child.

What to do

⑩ (10 mins) Introduction
Introduce the lesson to the whole class by talking generally about Egypt, the River Nile and its importance to the country (see 'Background information' on page 40).

Explain to the children the focus of the lesson:
- to use atlases, globes and maps to locate the River Nile, within the context of the world and in relation to the UK
- to use secondary sources of information to help label the features of the course of the River Nile
- to use the appropriate geographical vocabulary when describing the course of the River Nile.

㊺ (45 mins) Development
Using maps at a range of scales, children work in pairs to locate the positions of the United Kingdom, Europe, the Equator, the Tropics of Cancer and Capricorn, Africa, Egypt, the River Nile, Quesna, Cairo and Luxor. They should try to answer the following questions:
- Where is Africa in relation to Britain and Europe?
- Where is Egypt within Africa?
- How large is Egypt in comparison with the United Kingdom and Europe?
- What shape is Egypt?
- Which countries, seas and mountain ranges border Egypt?
- What physical features are there in Egypt, such as deserts, rivers and so on?
- Where are the River Nile and other major landmarks of Egypt located?
- Where is the source of the River Nile?
- Which countries does the River Nile flow through?
- Which sea does the River Nile flow into?
- Which way is the river flowing?

As a class, the children should then watch relevant parts of the BBC *Landmarks* video about Egypt – the programme entitled 'The Gift of the Nile' – and discuss what impact the River Nile has on the lives of the Egyptians (farming methods, heating and lighting in their homes, and so on).

Ask the children, working individually, to label the map of the River Nile on photocopiable page 126, from source to sea. They should use atlases, maps, reference books and other secondary sources to help them.

⑤ (5 mins) Plenary
At the end of the session, ask the children to describe the course of the River Nile. Have the children found out anything about the River Nile that has surprised them?

Differentiation
Less able children could be provided with simplified maps of the River Nile to label. Use human resources (classroom assistants/voluntary helpers), if available, to work with less able children.

CHAPTER 2
ECONOMICALLY
DEVELOPING
COUNTRIES

Egypt – a land
of surprises

More able children could use reference books and the Internet to find out about another river in another less-developed country.

Assessing learning outcomes

Ephemeral evidence

● Observation of, and listening to, the children as they work on the activities.

● Questions asked by the children and the answers given to questions framed by the teacher.

● Geographical vocabulary used by the children when discussing the course of the river.

Retainable evidence

● Children's completed photocopiable page 126.

ICT opportunities
Children use video evidence in this lesson. More able children could use the Internet as part of an extension activity.

Follow-up activity
Children could write an account of a journey along the Nile from source to mouth. They should name the countries it flows through, and describe the changing landscape, the animals that live in the river or on its banks, physical features they would see, and so on.

① 1 hour How do the Egyptians control the waters of the Nile?

What you need and preparation

You will need: atlases; maps of Egypt at different scales; BBC *Landmarks* video (programme entitled 'The Gift of the Nile'); *The Thread of the Nile* photopack (Teachers In Development Education, Development Education Centre, Birmingham, 1996, ISBN 0 948 83846 9), copies of photocopiable page 127, copied onto card and cut out (enough for each group to have a complete set); a copy of photocopiable page 128 for each child; information books about the Aswan Dam.

What to do

⑩ 10 mins Introduction

Introduce the lesson to the whole class by discussing why dams are built, and by giving the children some general information about the Aswan Dam, where it is situated and why it was built there (see 'Background information' on page 40).

Explain to the children the focus of the lesson:

● to ask geographical questions about how and why the Egyptians control the waters of the River Nile

● to collect, record and analyse evidence, and draw conclusions about the Aswan Dam and Lake Nasser

● to investigate the impact of the Aswan Dam on the processes of erosion and deposition downstream of the dam, and to review the effects that changes in the flow of the Nile are having on the land

● to investigate what impact the Aswan Dam has on the lives of the Egyptians (on their farming methods, heating and lighting in their homes, and so on)

● to identify and explain, in role, different views that people hold about the Aswan Dam

● to recognise how and why people may seek to manage environments in a sustainable way.

㊺ 45 mins Development

Children watch the relevant parts of the BBC *Landmarks* video, 'The Gift of the Nile', and use photographs from *The Thread of the Nile* photopack, reference books and the Internet to find out about the importance of the River Nile to the Egyptians. Using maps at a range of scales, children locate the Aswan Dam, Lake Nasser, Cairo and the river delta.

Learning objectives
● Ask geographical questions.
● Use appropriate geographical vocabulary.
● Use maps and plans at a range of scales.
● Locate the places and environments studied.
● Use secondary sources of information.
● Use ICT to help in geographical investigations.
● Collect and record evidence.
● Analyse evidence and draw conclusions.
● Investigate water and its effects on landscapes and people.
● Identify and explain different views that people, including themselves, hold about topical geographical issues.
● Recognise how and why people may seek to create and manage sustainable environments.
● Communicate in ways appropriate to the task and audience.

Lesson organisation
Teacher-led whole-class introduction to the Aswan Dam, after which children locate the places associated with the dam on maps at different scales; role-play activity in six mixed-ability groups of four to six children, followed by individual work writing newspaper reports. Whole-class plenary session at the end looking at possible future environmental and economic issues resulting from the building of the Aswan Dam.

Egypt – a land of surprises

Vocabulary
Aswan Dam
Lake Nasser
reservoir
mouth
source
delta
saline
salination
archaeological
fertile
fertilisers
agriculture
cash crops
erosion
deposition
irrigation
silt
earthquake
irrigation
channels
hydroelectric
power
climate
artificial lake
sustainable
environments

ICT opportunities
Children use evidence from video programmes in this lesson, and information from the Internet, to find out about the importance of the River Nile to the Egyptians.

Follow-up activity
Children could make a fact file on the Aswan Dam – the largest dam in the world – in which they compare it to another well-known dam; for example, the Hoover Dam.

Divide children into six mixed-ability groups, each assuming one of the following roles: farmers, government officials, environmentalists, industrialists, civil engineers, holiday company representatives, fishermen.

To help the children to understand their roles, ask them, in their groups, to discuss:
- Who are they?
- What job do they do?
- How do they spend most of their time?
- Are they rich or poor?
- How do they use the Nile for work?
- How do they use the Nile for pleasure?

Then ask each group, in role, to consider the positive benefits and negative effects of the Aswan Dam on their lives, using the cards from photocopiable page 127 to inform their discussions. Ask the children in each group to elect a spokesperson for the group.

Organise a mock public inquiry and allow each of the six representatives to speak for two minutes, presenting their view, in role.

Were some issues common to all groups? What were the greatest differences between groups and why?

After the discussion, ask the children to vote for or against the statement: 'The positive benefits of the Aswan Dam far outweigh any small negative effects it has had on the land and people of the Nile Valley.'

Ask the children to write a report on the positive benefits and negative effects of the Aswan Dam for the *Egyptian Daily News*, in the role of a reporter attending the public inquiry. They should use the writing frame on photocopiable page 128 to plan the article in their groups, but work individually to write their reports.

(5 mins) Plenary
At the end of the session, ask the children to reflect on the advantages and disadvantages of the Aswan Dam and what might need to be done in the future to reduce some of the problems that are beginning to develop.

Differentiation
All children have equal access to the discussion and debate, as they are working in mixed-ability groups.

Less able children could be provided with a simplified writing frame for their newspaper report. Use human resources (classroom assistants/voluntary helpers), if available, to work with less able children.

More able children could be asked to write the newspaper report without the aid of a writing frame.

Assessing learning outcomes
Ephemeral evidence
- Observation of, and listening to, the children's discussions as they carry out the activity.
- Questions asked by the children and the answers given to questions framed by the teacher.
- Geographical vocabulary used by the children when discussing and debating the issue.
- Children's critical use of evidence.
- Teamwork and co-operation – how well do the children work together in groups?

Retainable evidence
- Children's completed photocopiable page 128 and the newspaper reports they have written about the public enquiry.

CHAPTER 2
ECONOMICALLY
DEVELOPING
COUNTRIES

Egypt – a land
of surprises

Why is the River Nile important for tourism?

What you need and preparation

You will need: tourist brochures that include visits to Egypt and cruises on the River Nile; highlighter pens; access to the Internet; reference books and maps of Egypt; *The Thread of the Nile* photopack (TIDE, Development Education Centre, Birmingham (1996) ISBN 0 948 83846 9); *Cairo – Four Children and Their City* photopack (Oxfam); a copy of photocopiable page 129 for each child or group; display materials; access to computers with word-processing or DTP software.

The following suggestions may help the children when they are planning their itineraries.

Excursions on land:
- Aswan Dam and Lake Nasser
- Giza and the Pyramids
- Cairo
- Alexandria
- camel rides in the Sahara Desert
- a visit to a desert oasis
- watching camel racing
- Temples of Luxor
- alabaster craftsmen at work
- a visit to a market
- a ride on a felucca
- water sports.

Activities on-board ship:
- deck games
- sunbathing
- swimming
- disco/dinner dance
- banquets
- watching videos.

Further tourist information can be found on the Internet, at websites such as:

http://travel.yahoo.com/Destinations/Africa/Countries/Egypt/attract.html

http://travel.yahoo.com/Destinations/Africa/Countries/Egypt/facts.html

What to do

Introduction
(5 mins)
Explain to the children that tourism is very important to the modern Egyptian economy. Many tourists flock to the Nile and its immediate surrounding area because of Egypt's rich historical legacy.

Explain to the children the focus of the lesson:
- to investigate how the River Nile affects the lives of the Egyptian people and how they utilise the river as a tourist attraction
- to develop the correct geographical vocabulary to describe the Nile Valley and its immediate surroundings
- to use tourist brochures, maps and ICT to find the most up-to-date tourist information
- to produce their own brochure or display about a cruise holiday on the River Nile.

Development
(1 hour 5 mins)
Ask the children, in mixed ability-groups, to search tourist brochures and adverts for holidays

Egypt – a land of surprises

Vocabulary
tourism
economy
attraction
felucca
Aswan Dam
Lake Nasser
reservoir
archaeological
desert
cruise ship
deck games
on-shore activities

ICT opportunities
● Children could use the Internet to access the most up-to-date tourist information, including information about the weather, currency and tourist attractions.
● They could also use word-processing or DTP software to help present their display work or tourist brochure pages.

Follow-up activity
Children could discuss and debate the following question: *If you were Egyptian, how might you feel about the tourists on the cruise ships; particularly about the way they behave and dress?*

in Egypt and cruises on the Nile, to list all the places in Egypt that are visited by tourists, and to locate them on a map of Egypt. They should also look at and discuss the images illustrated in the brochures and adverts.

Ask the children to select an advert for a cruise or an article about a cruise on the River Nile, in pairs within the groups. Ask each pair to highlight in green the geographical vocabulary used in the advert and highlight in pink the descriptive words (both adjectives and adverbs). In their groups, they should then feed back some of the words they have highlighted and discuss their meanings. As a whole class, analyse and discuss the persuasive genre of writing used for advertising holidays.

Ask the children, back in their groups, to imagine they are on the Board of Directors of a holiday company, which owns a cruiser on the River Nile. The Board of Directors have to discuss the following items on the agenda of a board meeting:

1 On-board entertainment
What the passengers need on-board the cruise ship to keep them happy.

2 On-shore excursions
What the passengers require from the places at which the cruise ship stops – sightseeing excursions, souvenirs to buy, entertainment, and so on.

3 Items the cruise ship requires from stops in port
What items the cruise ship requires from the places at which it stops – fuel, water, food, and so on.

Ask the children to discuss the agenda items, in role, and to come up with some decisions and perhaps some action points regarding each item.

Still in the same groups, ask the children to design an itinerary for the cruise ship with eight attractions that would be part of the holiday. They should include some activities on-board ship as well as on-shore excursions to places of interest, markets, temples, and so on. Give the children photocopiable page 129 to help them plan, and access to the photopacks and other reference materials to help them decide upon possible sites for on-shore activities. The groups could use drawings or cut-out images from the tourist brochures to illustrate their written descriptions of the eight activities.

As a class, the children could then decide upon eight activities selected from all their ideas, and produce a display as described next. The teacher provides an outline of a Nile cruise ship on a large piece of paper. The children use images of places to visit in Egypt, cut out from tourist brochures, to fill the cruise ship outline and create a collage. The children, in mixed-ability groups of four to six, then select one of the chosen eight activities, and produce a large picture to describe it (using any medium), to go on the class display. Each group also provides a short piece of written information about their activity for the tourists.

Alternatively, the children could produce a class tourist brochure advertising the cruise with the chosen eight activities. Each group could work to produce a page in the brochure on one of the eight activities.

⏱ 5 mins Plenary
At the end of the lesson, have a general discussion to recap on the importance of the tourist industry to the Egyptian economy, linking the importance of the Nile in the past, the present and in the future.

Differentiation

All children have equal access to this activity, as they are working in mixed-ability groups.
Less able children might benefit from working with classroom assistants or voluntary helpers, if available.
More able children could use reference books and their own knowledge to discuss how the

CHAPTER 2
ECONOMICALLY
DEVELOPING
COUNTRIES

Egypt – a land
of surprises

local economy would be affected if the tourists stopped coming to Egypt. What sort of events or activities might lead to a decline in the number of tourists?

Assessing learning outcomes

Ephemeral evidence
- Observation of, and listening to, the children's discussions as they work on the activities.
- Geographical vocabulary used by the children when undertaking the activities.

Retainable evidence
- Children's completed photocopiable page 129.
- Class display or tourist brochure advertising the children's cruise.

What kinds of settlements are on the banks of the Nile?

1 hour 10 mins

What you need and preparation

In this lesson, el Beled is suggested as a village study. El Beled is based on villages in Upper Egypt near Qena. There is a wealth of information and photographs available in *The Thread of the Nile* photopack (TIDE, Development Education Centre, Birmingham, 1996, ISBN 0 948 83846 9). Maps of the village, information about people's daily lives, their homes, their jobs and the activities they do, education and health are all available.

El Quesna is suggested as a town study. On the BBC *Landmarks* video programme entitled 'Life in Cairo', there is a video clip featuring the Khalil family who live in Quesna, which is a market town on the delta near Cairo.

Cairo is suggested as a city study. Photographic and video evidence of the lifestyles of four children growing up here is available in the photopack *Cairo – Four Children and Their City* (Oxfam), and there is a lot of information on the Internet.

You will also need: copies of both parts of photocopiable page 130 (copied separately and enlarged) for each child; access to the Internet; atlases and maps of Egypt; reference books; *Ancient Lands* CD-ROM (Microsoft); *The Day of Ahmed's Secret* by F Parry (Gollancz, ISBN 0 140 56353 9).

What to do

Introduction
10 mins

Introduce the lesson with a general discussion to recap on the differences between settlement types, and the functions of settlements they have studied in the UK, including their own locality.

Explain to the children the focus of the lesson:
- to learn about different settlements along the banks of the River Nile, using maps, photographs, videos, reference books, the Internet, and so on
- to identify and describe what the different settlements are like, where they are and to explain why they are like they are
- to investigate how these settlements differ and change, including why they differ in size and character
- to recognise how these places fit within the wider geographical context and are interdependent.

As a class, decide on an Egyptian village, town and city to investigate and locate these settlements using atlases and maps.

Learning objectives
- Ask geographical questions.
- Collect and record evidence.
- Analyse evidence and draw conclusions.
- Communicate in ways appropriate to the task and audience.
- Use appropriate geographical vocabulary.
- Use secondary sources of information.
- Use ICT to help in geographical investigations.
- Identify and describe what places are like.
- Study maps at a range of scales.
- Locate the places and environments studied.
- Describe and explain how and why places are similar to and different from other places.
- Recognise how places fit within the wider geographical context and are interdependent.
- Investigate how settlements differ and change, including why they differ in size and character.

Lesson organisation
Teacher-led recap discussion on the functions of settlements. As a class, children decide on an Egyptian village, town and city to investigate and locate them. In three mixed-ability research groups, children investigate the village, town or city, using all available resources (maps, photographs, video, reference books, Internet). Working individually within groups, children carry out a settlement survey using photocopiable page 130, then create a fact file based on the second part of photocopiable page 130. In the same groups, using their fact files, children prepare and present a TV documentary.

Egypt – a land of surprises

Vocabulary
settlement
village
city
market
town
religious buildings
temple
farming
agriculture
cash crops
food crops
industry
high-rise flats
school
oasis
scrub land

ICT opportunities
Children could use the Internet to access the most up-to-date information about the settlements.

Follow-up activity
Children could compare and contrast the settlement their group studied in Egypt with a similar settlement in the UK (for example, compare Cairo with Manchester, Glasgow or Cardiff).

Development
50 mins Divide the class into three mixed-ability research groups. Each group should pick one of an Egyptian village, town or city to investigate. Ask the children, in their groups, to use all available resources relating to their settlement (maps, photographs, photopacks, video evidence, reference books, the Internet and so on) to undertake a settlement survey, and to create a fact file based on the information found, using both parts of photocopiable page 130.

Using their fact file, each group should prepare and present their information in the form of a documentary programme for children's TV, with interviews, reports and tourist information. The age of the intended audience is about 8 to 11 years.

Plenary
10 mins At the end of the lesson, have a general discussion to recap once again on the differences between the three settlement types studied.

Differentiation
All children have equal access to this activity, as they are working in mixed-ability groups. The creation of the TV documentary is an open-ended task, differentiated by outcome.

Less able children could use drawings to record information on photocopiable page 130, rather than written notes. Use human resources (classroom assistants/voluntary helpers), if available, to work with less able children.

Assessing learning outcomes
Ephemeral evidence
● Observation of, and listening to, the children's discussions as they carry out their research and work on their TV documentary.
● Geographical vocabulary used by the children when undertaking the activity.
● Teamwork and co-operation – how well do the children work together in groups?
Retainable evidence
● Children's completed photocopiable page 130 (settlement survey and fact file).

Water and its Effects on the Landscape

Introduction

This chapter has been designed to support the theme of 'water and its effects on landscapes...' (6c), as specified in the National Curriculum (2000) Programme of Study for Key Stage 2, in the Breadth of Study section. It also addresses 'how settlements differ and change...' (6d).

The four aspects of geography, as specified in the National Curriculum (2000) Programme of Study, can be taught through the theme of water in the landscape:

● **Geographical enquiry and skills** – for example, children ask geographical questions such as 'What is this landscape like?', 'What do I think about it?'

● **Knowledge and understanding of places** – for example, children identify and describe what physical landscapes are like and explain why they are like they are.

● **Knowledge and understanding of patterns and processes** – for example, children recognise physical processes such as river erosion, and explain how these can cause changes in places.

● **Knowledge and understanding of environmental change and sustainable development** – for example, children recognise how people can damage the environment (for example, by polluting a river) and identify opportunities for their own involvement in improving it.

Moving water is one of nature's most effective tools in the reshaping and remodelling of landscapes. Rivers, streams and the sea play a large part in altering the landscape, by rearranging and redistributing materials through the three processes of erosion, transportation and deposition.

Moving water creates a wide variety of different landscapes, depending on the rock type and the speed of the water. The physical environments so formed impact on the way the land may be used, and therefore on the lives of the people who live there. The way the land is used changes over the course of a river, reflecting the physical environment and landscape.

The 'Rivers' unit extends and amplifies Unit 14 'Investigating Rivers' in *A Scheme of Work for Key Stages 1 and 2* from the QCA. The final lesson described here concentrates on the physical processes at work in shaping a river valley, how the energy of the moving river water causes rocks to wear down (erode), and allows materials to be carried along (transported).

There is a wealth of resources available to support the delivery of the rivers element of 'water and its effects on landscapes...' (6c), including aerial photographs, ICT resources, and maps.

A visit to the local stream or river will bring the whole unit to life for children and give them the chance to undertake fieldwork activities (field sketches, data collection, investigations and so on), which are so vital to aid their understanding. The National Curriculum (2000) Programme of Study states that the themes are to be taught 'at a range of scales – local, regional and national' (7a); in 'different parts of the world' (7b) and include 'fieldwork investigations outside the classroom' (7c).

The second unit in this chapter is 'Investigating coasts', which may be studied as an alternative to 'Rivers', or combined with it (see below). The United Kingdom has nearly 18 000 kilometres of coastline, which represents a vast natural resource for schools. 'Investigating coasts' will open up many more environments – there are rocky shores, sandy bays and beaches, cliffs, headlands, sand dunes, salt marshes and many other marine environments for them to study.

There are also the physical processes that act upon coastal landscapes to investigate; for example, the ways in which the land is worn away (eroded) by the perpetual action of the waves and wind, as well as other elements of the weather. As well as wearing rocks away, the sea also carries (transports) sand, pebbles, stones and boulders, which are often deposited in the bays.

This 'Investigating coasts' unit has been written to support, supplement and extend the unit on 'Coasts' in the QCAs *A Scheme of Work for Key Stages 1 and 2*, and could also be linked with the National Curriculum for Science: 'Sc3 Materials and their Properties', 'Changing Materials' (2a-f).

Both the units in this chapter provide plenty of opportunities for work across the curriculum, including history, science, literacy, numeracy, sustainability, PSHE and citizenship. Lessons from both units could also be brought together to form a combined unit of work investigating the power of moving water on shaping the landscape and the impact of this on the lives of people.

Rivers

Background information

Rivers are among the main agents that shape our physical landscape, along with the sea, ice, wind and sun. In the past, rivers have had an enormous impact on people's lives, and continue to do so.

Rivers have been used in a variety of ways throughout history. At first rivers were used simply as a source of drinking water, as a source of food (fish) and as a means of transport. For convenience and safety, people tended to live above the flood level, but as near to a shallow, narrow part of the river as possible, to make crossing easy. People still use rivers as a source of water for drinking and transport, but with more sophisticated lifestyles, rivers are also used for the disposal of waste, both domestic and industrial, as well as in a multitude of industries (power generation, cooling, chemical manufacture, quarrying and extraction, paper making etc), and also for agriculture and leisure activities.

Water cycle

Before the children can begin to understand how a river system works, they need to have some understanding of the water cycle. It is essential that the children undertake practical work in both science and geography to gain an understanding of the basic principles of this cycle.

● **Water runs downhill:** ask the children to watch what happens when it rains. What happens to the rain when it hits a sloping roof? (Ask them to look at gutters, drainpipes and so on.) The ridge of the roof separates the way the water runs.

● **Evaporation:** ask the children to look at the puddles that form when it rains. Draw around the edge of a puddle with chalk at regular intervals (every 30 minutes) to plot shrinkage. This demonstrates that the puddle water returns to the air as vapour.

● **Cloud formation:** ask the children to look at the clouds. Explain that as the air (containing water vapour) rises it expands, becomes less dense and cools. This causes the water vapour to change back into water droplets.

● **Precipitation:** the droplets of water grow by joining together and eventually form drops that are heavy enough to fall out of the clouds as rain.

Journey of a river

Moving water has energy. The faster it moves the more energy it has. Rivers have energy, and they can wear things down, move things and carry them along as they flow. We call this the work of the river. The faster a river flows, the more energy it has and the more work it can do. Streams and rivers alter the landscape by redistributing material through the three processes of erosion, transportation and deposition (see opposite).

The start of a river is its source, which could be melting snow or ice, a spring (water bubbling out of the ground), a lake or a bog. The source of a river is usually in upland areas such as mountains or hills. Small streams flow downhill from the source and join other streams until they form the main river of a river system. The streams are the tributaries of the main river. In upland areas, water in streams and rivers is very fast-flowing, cutting and eroding the land to form valleys, and features such as waterfalls.

Where two streams join, or a stream joins a river, this is called a confluence. When the ground becomes flatter, the river slows down and starts to swing from side to side (meandering), making large bends (meanders). Sometimes, these large bends become cut off from the main river, and ox bow lakes are formed.

The end of a river, where it flows into the sea or sometimes a lake, is called its mouth. The area where the river meets the sea (the tidal part of the river) is called the estuary. A delta may be formed near the mouth of the river, if the land is very flat and the river is very slow-flowing and carrying a lot of sediment.

Erosion

Erosion is the wearing away and removal of natural material (rock, sand, soil) by a moving agent (in this case, running water). It is not water alone that erodes – the materials the water carries act as an abrasive tool, scouring the river bed and banks.

Rivers wear away the ground as they flow over it. They carve out valleys and shape the landscape. The shape that a river makes depends on how fast it flows and how hard the ground is.

There are three types of erosion:

● **Corrasion** is erosion caused by the physical impact of rocks on each other: when pebbles wear each other down it is called attrition; when pebbles and rocks scrape against and wearing away the bed and channel of the river, it is known as scouring or abrasion.

● **Corrosion** is erosion by solution (the water dissolves the rock).

● **Hydraulic** action is erosion caused by the sheer force of water (fracture).

Transportation

Rivers carry material in three ways:

● **Suspended load** – fine silt and clay is carried suspended in the water (in suspension).

● **Bedload** – when large particles, such as boulders, are rolled along the bed of the river, this is called traction; when small particles, such as sand, hop, bounce and skip along the bed, this is known as saltation.

● **Solute load** – rock material is carried dissolved in the water.

Deposition

The size of the pebbles found on the river bed depends on the speed of the flow of the river. Small sand particles are moved easily by slow-flowing water but it takes increasingly high speeds (more energy) to move gravel, pebbles and boulders. When the current weakens, the load is dropped (deposited), starting with the heaviest particles first.

There are certain points in a river's course where speed of flow is greater than at others. For example, in a meander the water runs faster on the outside of the bend than on the inside, so there is greater erosion on the outside of the bend. On the inside, there is more deposition and the particles carried in the water are smaller.

As the river gets nearer the sea, the ground is less steep, so the current is less strong and the river can no longer carry all the stones it has collected on its way. The river drops the stones on to the river bed. This is called deposition. When it reaches the flat land near the sea the river is carrying only very fine mud particles.

UNIT: Rivers

Enquiry questions	Teaching objectives	Teaching activities	Learning outcomes	Cross-curricular links
What are the features of a river? Where does the river start? Which places does it flow through?	● Ask geographical questions. ● Use appropriate geographical vocabulary. ● Use and draw maps and plans (plan of a river from source to the mouth). ● Use secondary sources of information (books, atlases, CD-ROMs, Internet). ● Recognise and explain patterns made by physical features in the environment. ● Investigate water and its effects on landscapes and people, including the physical features of rivers.	Children describe physical features of the course of the river using the correct geographical vocabulary; Children play 'River Snap' using cards produced from photocopiable page 131, use secondary sources of information to research definitions for river features, and label the diagram of a river from its source to its mouth, on photocopiable page 132.	Children: ● are able to use the correct geographical vocabulary for physical features of a river. develop awareness of the features of the whole river system.	
What are the main features and where does it meet the sea?	● Ask geographical questions. ● Use appropriate geographical vocabulary. ● Collect and record evidence. ● Use and draw maps and plans. ● Locate places and environments studied. ● Investigate water and its effects on landscapes and people, including the physical features of rivers. ● Recognise and explain patterns made by individual physical features.	Children match aerial photographs taken along the length of the river to points on an Ordnance Survey map (1:50 000), using four- or six-figure grid references. They also locate other main physical features and settlements and record grid references on photocopiable page 133.	● can use grid references to locate features of a river.	
How do we use rivers? How does the river change along its course? How and why does the use of the river and the surrounding land change over its course and time?	● Ask geographical questions. ● Use appropriate geographical vocabulary. ● Use secondary sources of information. ● Collect and record evidence. ● Use and draw maps. ● Investigate water and its effects on landscapes and people. ● Locate the places and environments studied.	Children brainstorm how rivers have been used since prehistoric times; Using the information collected in the previous lesson (on photocopiable page 133) and additional information from current Ordnance Survey maps, and aerial and ground photographs, children devise a key and record the main land-uses along the river under study; Children compare the current land-use with that shown on historical maps, and write a report (using word processing) identifying and explaining the major changes; Children can play 'The River Game' on photocopiable pages 134 and 135.	● can devise a key to record land-uses. ● can understand how and why land-uses change and how this affects the river system.	History: change of use over time
What causes river pollution? How does the type of land-use affect the river? Does it cause pollution?	● Ask geographical questions. ● Use appropriate geographical vocabulary. ● Collect and record evidence. ● Use maps. ● Use secondary sources of information. ● Investigate water and its effects on landscapes and people.	Children brainstorm and categorise the main types of water pollution. They read newspaper articles about events that have caused river pollution and discuss how they could be avoided in future; Children use the land-use data from the previous lesson to predict the types of pollution affecting the river studied, based on the activities occurring at points along its course. They also consider where pollution will be greatest, relating this to their land-use maps; Using photocopiable 136, children consider the threats posed by various forms of rubbish in rivers. They design a data-collection sheet to use when undertaking a rubbish survey of a local river, and discuss what actions they could take to improve matters.	● can predict and identify human activities that may cause pollution of the river.	Health education: health hazards of pollution ICT: spreadsheets and data collection. Literacy: writing letters to MPs etc. to campaign against pollution Citizenship: processes to improve water quality.
How do rivers shape the landscape? How do rivers work? How do the river bed and banks get worn away? How do rivers transport and deposit their loads?	● Ask geographical questions. ● Use appropriate geographical vocabulary. ● Investigate water and its effects on landscapes and people, including the physical features of rivers, and the processes of erosion and deposition that affect them. ● Recognise some physical and human processes and explain how these can cause changes in places and environments ● Communicate in ways appropriate to the task and audience.	Children discuss and describe the physical processes that have shaped the landscape i.e. the work of a river - erosion, transportation and deposition; On photocopiable 137, children answer questions about erosion, transportation and deposition, and complete a simple diagram to illustrate various methods of transportation.	● begin to understand how rivers shape the landscape. have some knowledge and understanding of complex terms describing the work of the river.	

Resources
Ground-level photographs of the features of a river; oblique aerial photographs of five different sites on the course of the river being studied; Ordnance Survey maps (1:50 000) and historical maps of the same area to locate aerial photographs; an outline base map (drawn by the teacher) of the course of the river being studied; dice and counters for 'River Game' (one per group); newspaper articles of accounts of real river pollution incidents, preferably that have occurred on the local river under study; copies of photocopiable pages 131–137 (page 131 to be copied onto card and cut out, pages 134 and 135 to be enlarged).

What are the features of a river?

What you need and preparation

You will need: two copies of the 'River Snap' cards from photocopiable page 131 for each group (copy the page on to card and cut out in advance); a copy of the river diagram on photocopiable page 132 for each child; ground-level photographs of river features (commercially produced photopacks are available).

What to do

Introduction

Explain to the children the focus of the lesson:
- to find out what the children already know about rivers
- to develop the correct geographical vocabulary to describe features of a river system.

Before introducing the theme of rivers, find out what children already know about river systems, and the terminology used to describe their features (see 'Background information', page 50). Introduce a simple baseline assessment by asking each child to write down their own definition of a river. Ask the children to discuss their definitions in pairs, and to list any words that they know to be connected to rivers. Then ask the children, in the same pairs, to draw a concept map to show how their words are connected to rivers.

Using photographs of river features, discuss, identify and name the features of a river as a whole class.

Development

Introduce the children to the game of 'River Snap'. Using two sets of cards from photocopiable page 131 for each group in the class (four children, of a mix of ability levels, in each group), the children play River Snap, following the rules for ordinary Snap (each group shuffling both sets of cards together). Children should call 'snap' when:
- two pictures of a feature match
- two names of a feature match
- a picture of a feature and a name match.

Ask the children, in pairs, to take each picture from the Snap game in turn, find the feature name that matches, and then write a definition for that feature using secondary sources (reference books, atlases, CD-ROMs, the Internet and so on). When the activity is completed, each pair should have a picture, a name and a definition for each feature. Additional photographic evidence may be provided by the teacher, to help the children define the terms.

Now that the children are more familiar with the names of the river features, ask them to label the diagram of a river from source to mouth on photocopiable page 132.

Plenary

At the end of the lesson, each pair feeds back to the rest of the class the information they have found out about each of the features. Together, the class produce a glossary of terms to put in their class book.

Differentiation

Children should work in mixed-ability groups, and so support each other. The 'River Snap' game is accessible to all, regardless of ability, and so encourages all children to be actively involved.

Less able children may benefit from working with classroom assistants or voluntary helpers, if available.

Learning objectives
- Ask geographical questions.
- Use appropriate geographical vocabulary.
- Use and draw maps and plans.
- Use secondary sources of information.
- Recognise and explain patterns made by individual physical features in the environment.
- Recognise some physical processes and explain how these can cause changes in places and environments.
- Investigate water and its effects on landscapes and people, including the physical features of rivers, and the processes of erosion and deposition that affect them.

Lesson organisation
Initial teacher introduction and simple assessment activities, followed by games in mixed-ability groups of about four children, then individual work on word definitions activity (written work) and diagram labelling activity; whole-class plenary session at the end.

Vocabulary
river
source
tributary
confluence
waterfall
meander
estuary
ox bow lake
delta
mouth

Rivers

ICT opportunities
See 'Follow-up activities', below.

Follow-up activity
Using atlases on a CD-ROM (for example, Encarta – The Complete Interactive Multimedia Encyclopedia, from Microsoft), or on the Internet, children could find diagrams and photographs of complete river systems (for example, the River Severn, River Rhine or the River Ganges). They could locate and name the sources of these rivers, and the places where they enter the sea. Children could select one of these rivers and find out about its physical features and its impact on the people who live along its banks.

More able children may be given additional geographical vocabulary associated with the river to illustrate and define.

Assessing learning outcomes
Ephemeral evidence
● Observation of, and listening to, the children's discussions amongst themselves when undertaking the activities
● Children's ability to understand and play the 'River Snap' game
● Geographical vocabulary used by children when undertaking the activities
● Teamwork and co-operation – how well do the children work together in groups and in pairs?
Retainable evidence
● Each child's initial definition of a river
● The concept maps drawn by pairs of children
● Glossary of definitions produced by each pair

How does the river change along its course?

Learning objectives
● Ask geographical questions.
● Use appropriate geographical vocabulary.
● Use secondary sources of information.
● Collect and record evidence.
● Use and draw maps and plans.
● Locate the places and environments studied.
● Investigate water and its effects on landscapes and people, including the physical features of rivers, and the processes of erosion and deposition that affect them.
● Recognise and explain patterns made by individual physical features in the environment.
● Recognise some physical processes and explain how these can cause changes in places and environments.

Lesson organisation
Initial teacher-led discussion with whole class, followed by group enquiry activity; children to work in five mixed-ability groups of approximately six children; whole-class plenary session at the end. Groups work on the photographs and maps for each site in turn (round robin).

What you need and preparation
You will need: oblique aerial photographs of five different sites along the course of the river being studied (commercially produced photopacks are available); Ordnance Survey maps (1:50 000) of the same area to locate features shown in aerial photographs; five copies per group of photocopiable page 133 (one for each site); word bank of river vocabulary to help the less able children.

What to do
10 mins **Introduction**
Introduce the lesson to the whole class by revising some of the geographical vocabulary used to describe the course of a river from source to mouth (see 'Background information', page 50). Find out what the children know about rivers and their uses by asking questions such as:
● Where do rivers come from?
● Where do rivers go?
● What makes a river valley?
● Where is this river located?
● How do we cross the river?
● Who uses rivers?
● How do people use rivers?
● Why do we pollute rivers?

Discuss what is meant by the terms 'physical (natural) features', 'human features', 'land-use' and 'transport'.

Explain to the children the focus of the lesson:
● to use aerial photographs and maps to identify human and physical features and land-use at selected sites along the course of a river
● using this information, to describe how the land-use changes over the distance from the source to the mouth of a river
● to locate the positions of the aerial photographs using four- or six-figure grid references.

Rivers

Recap by asking the children what an oblique aerial photograph is. Show the children the oblique aerial photographs to be used in the activity, and explain that each photograph shows a place along the course of the river.

🕐50mins Development

The children should work in mixed-ability groups. Each group studies oblique aerial photographs of each of the five sites along the river to identify the physical features, human features, land-use and transport at each site. In groups, the children discuss how they feel about the area, and what the river is like, at each site. They should think about who uses the river, and what it is used for. On the map of the river, they locate the area shown in the photograph using four- or six-figure grid references. They can also get additional information about each site by studying the map, and can record their findings on a copy of photocopiable page 133.

The groups spend about ten minutes, on each site, then move on to look at the photograph and map of the next site, recording their findings on a fresh copy of photocopiable page 133.

🕐15mins Plenary

At the end of the lesson, groups feed back the information they have found out about the river to the rest of the class.

Differentiation

Less able children could be given word lists of geographical vocabulary to help them to identify the features shown in the photographs. Use some of the words listed in the 'Vocabulary' section, left, as appropriate to the ability of the children, and also include words specific to the river being studied. Ask the children to match the words to what they can see in each photograph. Provide less able children with simpler maps than Ordnance Survey maps and ask them to use co-ordinates instead of grid references.

Use human resources (classroom assistants/voluntary helpers), if available, to work with less able children.

More able children could try to locate similar features on maps of different river systems using six-figure grid references. Using the aerial photographs and maps, more able children could write a description of the course of the river from source to mouth.

Assessing learning outcomes

Ephemeral evidence

- Observation of the children undertaking the activity, and discussion with them.
- Questions asked by the children and answers given to questions framed by the teacher.
- Geographical vocabulary used by the children when undertaking the activity.
- Teamwork and co-operation – how well do the children work together in groups?

Retainable evidence

- Children's completed photocopiable page 133, showing: Identification of river features from photographs and maps and the use of four- or six-figure grid references (or co-ordinates).

Vocabulary
river
stream
source
tributary
confluence
waterfall
meander
estuary
channel
delta
mouth
lake
reservoir
dam
flood plain
erosion
deposition
transportation
hill
mountain
valley
human feature
physical feature

Follow-up activity
Practical fieldwork: children could observe, describe and record the features of a river, using labelled field sketches. They could collect data about the direction, speed of flow, and temperature of the water. They could measure and draw the river channel, and record signs of pollution. Children could use environmental indicators (stream life) to record water quality.

Rivers

① How do we use rivers?
hour

Learning objectives
● Ask geographical questions.
● Use appropriate geographical vocabulary.
● Use secondary sources of information.
● Collect and record evidence.
● Use and draw maps.
● Investigate water and its effects on landscapes and people.
● Locate the places and environments studied.

Lesson organisation
Initial teacher introduction followed by simple brainstorming activity. Then children work in the same mixed-ability groups of about six as in the previous lesson ('How does the river change along its course?'), to record land-uses on a base map, and work in groups of four to six to play 'The River Game' (photocopiable pages 134 and 135); whole-class plenary session at the end.

Vocabulary
industry
sewerage
extraction industry
power
pollution

What you need and preparation
You will need: current Ordnance Survey maps (1:50 000) showing the river being studied; historical maps of the river (available from your local Records Office); aerial and ground-level photographs of the river; children's completed photocopiable pages 133, from the previous lesson, 'How does the river change along its course?' (page 54); an outline base map (drawn by the teacher) of the course of the river being studied; sufficient dice (one per group), coloured counters and copies of 'The River Game' (photocopiable pages 134) for groups of four to six children to play.

What to do
⑩ Introduction
mins
Explain to the children the focus of the lesson:
● to develop an understanding of the importance of rivers through history
● to recognise that a river can provide many opportunities for both transport and land-use and that these activities change over time and over the course of the river
● to consider how human activities (such as navigation, building, farming, industry and pollution) affect the river in different ways and how different groups help to manage and care for rivers
● to record information about current land-use along the course of the river on a base map of the river, and to add any additional information from Ordnance Survey maps, and aerial and ground - level photographs
● to compare current land-uses with land-uses shown on historical maps and to try to explain the changes that are evident.

Ask the children, in mixed-ability groups, to brainstorm how rivers have been used throughout history from prehistoric times to the present day (see 'Background information', page 50). Ask the children to draw a timeline and place the activities in order.

㊵ Development
mins
Ask the children, in the same mixed-ability groups as the previous lesson ('How does the river change along its course?', page 54), to record the information about current land-use along the course of the river that they collected in the previous lesson (recorded on photocopiable page 133) on a base map of the river provided by the teacher. Then they should add any additional information that they can find from Ordnance Survey maps, aerial and ground-level photographs, and devise a key to show the different land-uses.

Ask the children to list any changes in land-use that are evident, using historical maps, and to suggest possible reasons for the changes. Each group should produce a short report, and then feed back to the whole class.

Introduce the children to 'The River Game' on photocopiable pages 134 and 135. Explain the rules of the game. Up to a maximum of six children can play. Each player takes turns to throw the dice. A player must throw a six to start. If a player lands on a square with an issue, he or she must read the issue out to the group, discuss the issue and follow the instructions. The first player to reach 100 is the winner.

⑩ Plenary
mins
At the end of the lesson, ask the children about land-use along the course of the river, and how it changes from the source to the mouth. Ask the children to predict reasons for this and to think about sources of pollution.

Differentiation

Less able children should be provided with a base map of the river that includes more detail; for example, the zones of different land-use could be marked on, so that children just have to label them with the correct land-use. 'The River Game' is accessible to all, regardless of ability, and so encourages all children to be actively involved. Use human resources (classroom assistants/voluntary helpers), if available, to work with less able children.

More able children could undertake some research about an industry that used to operate on the banks of the river and now no longer does so. The children should concentrate on the reasons the industry was sited on the riverbank and the reasons why it is no longer operating there.

Assessing learning outcomes

Ephemeral evidence

● Observation of, and listening to, the children's discussion while they play 'The River Game'.
● Geographical vocabulary used by the children when undertaking the activity.
● Teamwork and co-operation – how well do the children work together in groups and play the game?

Retainable evidence

● The children's timelines of the uses of the river through history.
● The children's completed base maps of current land-use.
● The children's report on the changes of land-use through history.

> **Follow-up activity**
> Children could undertake some research (using reference books and the Internet), to find out about a modern industry that utilises the river and its water in its operations.

What causes river pollution?

What you need and preparation

You will need: newspaper articles of accounts of real river pollution incidents (if possible, incidents affecting the river the children are studying) – for example, incidents involving oil spillage from a pipeline into the river, slurry from a pig farm, droughts, floods, raw sewage being discharged into a river, waste from mines poisoning rivers, speedboats on rivers, shopping trolleys in rivers and so on; a copy of photocopiable page 136 for each child; land-use maps produced in the previous lesson, 'How do we use rivers?'.

What to do

15 mins Introduction
Explain to the children the focus of the lesson:

● to consider how human activities (such as navigation, building, farming, industry and pollution) affect the river in different ways; human activities can cause river pollution
● to understand that people can have positive, as well as negative, effects on river systems, and how different groups help to manage and care for rivers
● using evidence from the land-use maps produced in the previous lesson, to predict the type(s) of pollution that might affect the river they are studying, and to identify where they think pollution will be highest
● to learn how they, both collectively and as individuals, may help to protect the river system.

Water is used in a multitude of industries (power generation, cooling, chemical manufacture, quarrying and extraction, paper making, and so on), and also for agriculture and leisure. Some activities, if they are not managed correctly, may cause water to become polluted.

As a whole class, brainstorm the main types of water pollution. Categorise the types under the headings of 'Industrial Pollution', 'Sewage', 'Farming' and 'Rubbish/Litter'.

> **Learning objectives**
> ● Ask geographical questions.
> ● Use appropriate geographical vocabulary.
> ● Collect and record evidence.
> ● Use maps.
> ● Use secondary sources of information.
> ● Investigate water and its effects on landscapes and people.
>
> **Lesson organisation**
> Initial teacher introduction followed by simple brainstorming activity; in mixed-ability groups, children then carry out an activity based on newspaper articles (photocopiable page 136), predict types and locations of river pollution based on land-use data, produce a data-collection sheet for a river pollution survey, and discuss how to improve their local river; whole-class plenary session at the end.
>
> **Vocabulary**
> industry
> sewage
> pollution

Rivers

Follow-up activities
• Fieldwork: visit a local stream and undertake a survey of biological indicators to find out how clean or polluted the water is. Children could use spreadsheets to analyse and present the data collected. The children may wish to write to their local MP or the Environment Agency expressing their concerns.
• Read *The World that Jack Built* by R Brown (Red Fox Picture Books, ISBN 0 099 78960 4), which focuses on industrial pollution. The story follows the journey of a cat from an idyllic cottage that 'Jack' built, past the clean stream, over the rolling hills and through the woods. As we get further away from the cottage, the idyll fades. We find a polluted stream, a place where trees can no longer grow. Eventually we find that this is the world 'next to the factory that Jack built'. Ask the children to list the similarities and differences between the stream that flows past Jack's house and the one by Jack's factory. Organise a role-play activity, in which children put themselves into Jack's shoes and answer questions from the other children, in role. This 'I'd like to ask Jack...' activity helps to develop questioning skills. (Although Jack doesn't feature in the story, he could make an appearance in this kind of activity.) The children could ask him questions about his home, his factory, his attitude to the environment and to the future. Is there anything Jack could do about the pollution?

⏱ 50 mins Development
Ask the children to read the newspaper articles about river pollution incidents. Working in mixed-ability groups, children should select one article on which to focus, and discuss how the pollution of the river occurred and how it might be avoided in the future.

Using evidence from the land-use maps produced in the previous lesson ('How do we use rivers?', page 56), children suggest what types of pollution might affect the river at different points along its length, and where they think pollution will be greatest, based on the kinds of activities that occur at different points along the river's course.

Ask the children to focus on rubbish abandoned by people in rivers (unwanted items, broken items, discarded packaging, litter). In groups, they should list four reasons why litter and rubbish in the river is a bad thing. Then they should list four reasons why pollution of the river by litter and rubbish is everyone's problem. Ask each group to record how dangerous they feel different types of rubbish are, using photocopiable page 136.

Children then design a data-collection sheet that could be used when surveying the litter and rubbish found in the local river. If possible, a real visit to the local river to collect such data would be extremely helpful. When collected, the children can then analyse and present their data using spreadsheet software.

Ask the children what they think can be done to improve their local river. Ensure the children understand that everyone can do something to help. Ask the children to discuss, in groups, what they feel they can do, either as individuals or as a group. Children may come up with ideas such as writing to the local MP, council or Mayor, or getting their parents to work with them to undertake a stream 'clean-up campaign' (in this case, health and safety considerations must be emphasised), or they may want to investigate the causes of the pollution further upstream and then write to the Environment Agency, for example.

Photocopiable page 136 suggests that children write a newspaper article about the problem of rubbish polluting the local river; if the children have investigated a real pollution problem at a real river site, they could send their articles to the local newspaper to bring the issue to the public's attention. Similarly, if they are concerned about a real issue, they could actually send their letters to the local MP, council or Mayor, or take steps to start up a real clean-up campaign.

⏱ 10 mins Plenary
Discuss with the children what actions, if any, they could take to improve the condition of the river and to protect it from pollution. Encourage them to act as responsible citizens. Discuss the visit to the local stream or river and their data-collection sheets.

Differentiation
Less able children could use drawings rather than written responses to answer questions 2 and 3 on photocopiable page 136.

More able children could use secondary sources, including the Internet, to research river pollution around the world.

Assessing learning outcomes
Ephemeral evidence
● Observation of, and listening to, children's discussion of how pollution may be avoided.
● Ideas arising from the brainstorming activity on types of pollution.
Retainable evidence
● The children's completed photocopiable page 136.
● The children's data-collection sheets.

 How do rivers shape the landscape?

What you need and preparation

You will need: a copy of photocopiable page 137 for each child.

What to do

Introduction

Explain to the children the focus of the lesson:

- to investigate water and its effects on landscapes and people, including the physical features of rivers
- discuss and describe the physical processes that have shaped the landscape
- to investigate the effects of the processes of erosion, transportation and deposition on rivers.
  Introduce the lesson by discussing the energy of moving water and the work of the river (that is, the three processes of erosion, transportation and deposition – see 'Background information' on page 50). Ask the children to complete questions 1, 2 and 3 on photocopiable page 137.

Development
Erosion section on photocopiable page 137

Whole-class discussion of the process of erosion, and then children complete the erosion section, working individually.

Transportation section on photocopiable page 137

Whole-class discussion about transportation, and then children work on the transportation section on their own.

Deposition section on photocopiable page 137

Whole-class discussion on deposition, and then children complete the deposition section.

Ask the children to write a short, vivid description about the work of a river, in the role of a small pebble that is transported from the source to the mouth of the river.

Plenary

At the end of the lesson, discuss the work of the river with the children and ask some of them to read out their descriptive passages.

Learning Objectives
- Ask geographical questions.
- Use appropriate geographical vocabulary.
- Investigate water and its effects on the landscapes and people, including the physical features of rivers, and the processes of erosion and deposition that affect them.
- Recognise some physical and human processes and explain how these can cause changes in places and environments.
- Communicate in ways appropriate to the task and audience.

Lesson Organisation
Initial teacher introduction about the energy of moving water and the work of the river (the processes of erosion, deposition and transportation), followed by discussion and activity on deposition; whole-class plenary session at the end.

Vocabulary
erosion
transportation
deposition
traction
attrition
saltation
abrasion
suspension
corrasion
corrosion
hydraulic action
river bed

Rivers

Follow-up activity
● Children could make up a dance about the work of the river (erosion, transportation and deposition) using appropriate movements to imitate the river.
● Children could listen to a piece of music called 'Vltava' by Smetana. This piece of music follows the course of the River Vltava from its source, through Prague, to the sea. You can feel the change in the power of the river with the changes in the music.

Differentiation

Less able children could be asked to describe the work of the river in their own words with diagrams, rather than completing photocopiable page 137. Use human resources (classroom assistants/voluntary helpers), if available, to work with less able children.

More able children could work in groups to identify the sort of work they think the river is doing in photographs provided by the teacher.

Assessing learning outcomes

Ephemeral evidence

● Observation of, and listening to, children's responses to the teacher's questioning.

Retainable evidence

● The children's completed photocopiable 137.

Investigating coasts

Background information

The United Kingdom has nearly 18 000 kilometres of coastline and nowhere in the UK is more than 160 kilometres from the sea. As a result, the seaside is a popular place for holidays and days out. This unit will open up some of the wonders of the UK's landscapes to children as there are so many different marine environments for them to study, including rocky shores, sandy bays and beaches, cliffs, headlands, sand dunes and salt marshes.

Bays and headlands occur along parts of the coast and are found where different types of rock come into contact with the sea. Some rock is more resistant to attack from the sea and the processes of erosion than others. Hard rocks are usually more resistant and so stick out as cliffs and headlands, while softer rocks are worn away (eroded) to form bays. For example, because limestone is more resistant than slate and shale, where these rocks occur at the coast the limestone forms headlands while the more easily eroded slate and shale forms a bay – as in the Great Orme, Llandudno.

Cliffs are under continual attack from waves and wind, as well as from other elements of the weather. They are undercut by wave action and sometimes this makes them unstable. Eventually, after many, many years, some parts of the cliffs (for example, overhanging rocks) may collapse and fall as large boulders. Caves may form where the incoming waves hurl themselves against weak points in the cliffs and erode the rock more quickly than elsewhere. If two caves on opposite sides of a headland back into each other, an arch may be formed – for example, Durdle Door in Dorset. If erosion continues, eventually the roof of the arch may collapse, leaving rocks sticking out in the sea. These isolated rocks are called stacks; examples include the Needles on the Isle of Wight and the Old Man of Hoy in the Orkneys.

As well as wearing away rocks, the sea also carries sand, pebbles and stones. These are often dumped (deposited) in bays, which forms beaches. This happens because the waves have less energy by the time they reach the bay and can no longer carry their load. There are many different kinds of beaches: the main ones are sandy, rocky, muddy and shingle. Beaches provide habitats for different animals and plants.

Some of the finer rock particles may be transported to deeper, quieter waters (for example, the mouth of a river or a bay), where they may be deposited. Over time, the deposited material builds up to form a spit of newly formed land across the bay or river – Spurn Head at the mouth of the River Humber is an example of a spit. If a spit becomes so long that it reaches right across an indentation in the coastline, it is known as a bar. For example, Chesil Bank in Dorset is a sixteen-mile long shingle bar, linking the 'Isle' of Portland to the mainland.

UNIT: Investigating coasts

Enquiry questions	Teaching objectives	Teaching activities	Learning outcomes	Cross-curricular links
What does this coastline look like? Which coastal environments have I visited? Where are these places located? What are the main physical features of different coastal environments? What are the main human features?	• Use atlases, globes and maps at a range of scales. • Use secondary sources of information. • Identify and describe what places are like. • Locate the places and environments studied. • Describe and explain how and why places are similar to and different from others. • Investigate water and its effects on landscapes and people, including the physical features of coasts, and the processes of erosion and deposition that affect them. • Recognise some physical and human processes and explain how these can cause changes in places and environments.	Children talk about coastal environments they have visited in the UK and beyond, focusing on the physical and human features, as they perceived them from their visit; Children select one coastal location they have visited, locate it in an atlas and mark it on an interactive class display; Children draw a postcard, from memory, including the main characteristics of their chosen place, to add to the display; Using six photographs of coastal environments, selected by the teacher, children discuss similarities and differences, both in terms of physical and human features and the processes leading to their formation (see photocopiable page 138).	Children: • use grid references to locate beaches. • develop awareness of the features of coasts. • can devise a key to record physical features and environments.	
Why does this coastline look like this? How and why do the physical features of coasts relate to the underlying rock type? Which features are characteristic of hard and soft rock?	• Ask geographical questions. • Use appropriate geographical vocabulary. • Use secondary sources of information. • Collect and record evidence. • Investigate water and its effects on landscapes and people, including the physical features of coasts, and the processes of erosion and deposition that affect them. • Recognise some physical processes and explain how these can cause changes in places and environments.	Children brainstorm what they know about erosion, and discuss erosion in general terms. Children read how rock hardness affect the formation of coastal landscapes, and then sort different rock types according to 'hardness' (photocopiable page 139). They also sort rocks according to whether they have been smoothed and rounded by attrition on a beach; Children discuss specific ways in which the coastline is being eroded (worn away) ie the processes of erosion. They investigate some of the processes of erosion, by undertaking some experiments, as described on photocopiable page 139.	• can identify different rocks and sort according to hardness. • understand some of the processes of erosion acting on coastlines.	Science: Sc3 materials and their properties – grouping and classifying.
What are these coastal features called? What are caves, arches and stacks? How are they formed and why?	• Locate places and environments studied. • Use secondary sources of information. • Investigate water and its effects on landscapes, including the physical features of coasts, and the processes of erosion and deposition that affect them. • Recognise some physical processes and explain how these can cause changes in places and environments.	Using photocopiable page 140, children label and write captions for a field sketch of a headland area where caves, arches and stacks are evident. Children look at series of drawings showing the development of a stack, on photocopiable page 140, and describe what they think has happened and why. Children locate examples of these features on maps.	• can use appropriate geographical vocabulary to label features and to describe the agents and processes of erosion.	Art: sketches
What is this coastal settlement like? What are the different characteristics of the sites chosen for different economic activities? Do all European countries have a coastline?	• Collect and record evidence. • Communicate in ways appropriate to the task and audience. • Use secondary sources of information. • Use ICT. • Learn about similarities and differences between places. • Identify and describe what places are like. • Locate the places and environments studied. • Investigate water and its effects on landscapes and people. • Investigate how settlements differ and change.	Children brainstorm uses of different coastal areas in the UK and Europe, and then list the European countries that have no coastline. Children locate various places on maps of the UK and Europe; In small groups, children research one of these locations using the Internet, CD-ROMs, maps and reference books. What are the main economic activities of each place? How have these places changed over time? Children record their findings on photocopiable page 141. When groups feed back to the class, the children discuss how the places they have studied are similar and different.	• show a developing understanding of coastal features and processes. • can use secondary sources of information • communicate research in an appropriate way. • gain an understanding of the different functions of coastal settlements.	ICT: using the Internet and CD-ROMs for research.
Where do people go on holiday? Where do people choose to take their holidays in the UK?	• Collect and record evidence. • Analyse evidence and draw conclusions. • Communicate in ways appropriate to the task and audience. • Use atlases and globes, and maps at a range of scales. • Use secondary sources of information. • Use ICT. • Use decision-making skills. • Identify and describe what places are like. • Locate the places and environments studied. • Investigate water and its effects on landscapes and people.	As a class, children produce a travel brochure illustrating different holiday destinations in the UK for people who require different types of coastal holidays (eg beach holiday, rock climbing, etc). In groups of two or three, children use the Internet, CD-ROMs, maps and reference books to locate a suitable place in the UK to satisfy different a certain client profile (photocopiable page 142). They describe and illustrate the holiday destinations for the class brochure. Using the role-play cards on photocopiable page 143, children select a holiday from the class travel brochure, in role, and give reasons for their choice.	• gain an understanding of the holiday requirements of different people.	

Resources
Card and drawing materials to make 'postcards'; large wall map of the world; six photographs of different coastal environments, showing a range of human and physical features; a mixture of hard and soft rocks, such as pieces of chalk, sandstone, limestone, slate (Sample A); mixture of rocks and pebbles, some from the beach and some from the elsewhere (Sample B); small pieces of limestone or chalk; vinegar; small plastic bottles (not glass); water; access to a deep freeze; small pieces of sandstone, limestone and chalk soaked in water overnight; photographs of coastal features caused by erosion (from magazines, calendars etc); Ordnance Survey maps of areas showing coastal features; wall map of the UK; maps of the UK and Europe; photographs of the different coastal settlements; tourist brochures for British seaside holidays and specialist holidays (for example, birdwatching); twelve photocopies of the class holiday brochure (when the children have produced it); ICT hardware and software (CD-ROMs); access to the Internet; atlases, maps and other reference books; copies of photocopiable pages 138 to 141 for each child; photocopiable pages 142 and 143 copied onto card and cut out.

Display
Interactive display of coastal locations visited – large wall map of the world with children's 'postcards' used to label the resorts, class holiday brochure.

Investigating
coasts

1 hour — What does this coastline look like?

What you need and preparation

You will need: atlases and maps; card and drawing materials to make postcards; large wall map of the world for class display of coasts visited by the children; six photographs of different coastal environments, carefully selected by the teacher to show a range of human and physical features; a copy of photocopiable page 138 for each child.

What to do

15 mins Introduction

Introduce the lesson by asking what coastal environments the children have visited in the UK and beyond, and what physical and human features they remember from their visits. Discuss, in general terms, the processes that affect coastal areas to create different landforms.

The physical features of a coastline exert a considerable influence on the human activities that take place on that coast. The UK has a very wide and varied coastline with some unique physical features and a wide variety of human activities. Headlands provide shelter for bays; bays are good sites for villages, towns and ports. For example, the headlands of The Great Orme and The Little Orme provide shelter for the bay at Llandudno.

Explain to the children the focus of the lesson:
- to investigate similarities and differences in coastal environments
- to discuss and describe the physical processes that have shaped the coast
- to learn about the physical features of coasts and the processes of erosion and deposition that affect them
- to locate different coastal environments on maps.

35 mins Development

Ask the children to each select one coastal location that they have visited, and to locate this place in an atlas or on a map. Create an interactive class display by asking each child to indicate where their coastal location is on a large wall map of the world. Then ask the children to draw a postcard, from their memory, which includes the main characteristics of their chosen place to add to the interactive class display.

Working in six mixed-ability groups of five or six children, depending on the size of the class, the children discuss the similarities and differences between six coastal environments from the photographs provided by the teacher, both in terms of physical and human features and the processes leading to their formation. Then, individually, each member of the group completes photocopiable page 138.

10 mins Plenary

At the end of the lesson, discuss with the whole class:
- Which two places in the photographs were the most similar in terms of physical features?
- Which two places in the photographs were the most similar in terms of human features?
- Which two places in the photographs were the most different in terms of physical features?
- Which two places in the photographs were the most different in terms of human features?

Learning objectives
- Ask geographical questions.
- Use appropriate geographical vocabulary.
- Collect and record evidence.
- Use and draw maps.
- Use atlases, globes and maps at a range of scales.
- Use secondary sources of information.
- Identify and describe what places are like.
- Locate the places and environments studied.
- Describe and explain how and why places are similar to and different from other places.
- Investigate water and its effects on landscapes and people, including the physical features of coasts, and the processes of erosion and deposition that affect them.
- Recognise some physical and human processes and explain how these can cause changes in places and environments.

Lesson organisation
Teacher-led discussion about coasts visited by the children and the physical processes that affect coastal areas; individual work locating coasts and drawing postcards to add to a class display. Then children work in six mixed-ability groups of five or six, to record features of six coastal environments (from photographs) on photocopiable page 138, and discuss similarities and differences; whole-class plenary session at the end.

Vocabulary
human features
physical features
bay
headland
cliff
beach
sea
shore
groyne
hotels
apartments
amusements
arcades
hill
mountain
shops

CHAPTER 3
WATER AND ITS
EFFECTS ON THE
LANDSCAPE

Investigating
coasts

**Follow-up
activity**
Children could
plan a new seaside
resort, which has
everything that is
required for a
seaside holiday.
They should think
carefully about
what physical
features the ideal
coastal location for
their resort should
have.

Differentiation

This lesson is accessible to children of all abilities. All the work is undertaken in mixed-ability groups.

Less able children may benefit from working with human resources (classroom assistants/ voluntary helpers), if available.

More able children could draw and label a 'field' sketch of the coastal environment in one of the photographs.

Assessing learning outcomes

Ephemeral evidence

● Observation of, and listening to, children working in groups on the activity.

● Responses to the teacher's questioning.

Retainable evidence

● The children's completed photocopiable page 138.

 ## Why does this coastline look like this?

Learning objectives
● Ask geographical questions.
● Use appropriate geographical vocabulary.
● Use secondary sources of information.
● Collect and record evidence.
● Investigate water and its effects on landscapes and people, including the physical features of coasts, and the processes of erosion and deposition that affect them.
● Recognise some physical processes and explain how these can cause changes in places and environments.

Lesson organisation
Initial teacher introduction and simple assessment activity; whole-class discussion about erosion in general, then children work in six mixed-ability groups of five or six, naming and categorising rocks. Then follows a whole-class discussion on the processes of erosion and the children set up experiments. The experiments have to be left for at least 24 hours. Finally, whole-class plenary session about the outcome of each experiment and its link with erosion on coastal areas.

What you need and preparation

You will need: two samples of rock for each group – Sample A (a mixture of hard and soft rocks; for example, pieces of chalk, sandstone, limestone, slate etc) and Sample B (a mixture of rocks and pebbles, some from the beach and some from elsewhere); small pieces of limestone or chalk for each group; vinegar; a small plastic (not glass) bottle for each group; water; access to a deep-freeze; small pieces of sandstone, limestone and chalk that have already been soaked in water overnight; a copy of photocopiable page 139 for each child.

General information about the experiments (as described on photocopiable page 139):

Experiment 1 – children are asked to classify each rock in Sample A as 'hard' or 'soft', and if possible to name them. (Answers will depend on the rocks the teacher provides.)

Experiment 2 – children are asked to say which rocks in Sample B came from the beach. A piece of rock from the beach is smooth and rounded; it has been worn smooth by the continual tumbling and rubbing action as the water jostles the pebbles against each other

Experiment 3 – children stand a small piece of chalk or limestone in vinegar: the mixture will fizz as carbon dioxide is given off. If enough vinegar is used, the chalk and limestone will eventually dissolve away.

Experiment 4 – children fill a small plastic bottle with water and leave it in a deep-freeze overnight (the bottle must be plastic, must be filled completely, and the lid must be screwed on tightly): when the water freezes, it expands as it turns to ice, splitting the bottle.

Experiment 5 – children put small pieces of water-saturated sandstone, chalk and limestone into a deep-freeze overnight: when water-saturated rocks freeze, the water in them expands as it turns to ice, causing the cracks in them to widen so that the rocks crumble

What to do

10 mins **Introduction**
Explain to the children the focus of the lesson:

● to find out what they already know about erosion

● to undertake some practical experiments to illustrate some of the effects of erosion on different types of rock

● to develop the correct geographical vocabulary to describe the agents and processes of erosion

**Investigating
coasts**

● to develop knowledge and understanding of the processes of erosion on a coastal location and their effects on the landscape.

Before starting the investigation into erosion, find out what the children already know about the process. Undertake a simple baseline assessment by asking the children to write down anything they know about coastal erosion.

Development

Begin with a class discussion about what erosion actually means and what is being eroded. Ask the children, in mixed ability groups, to read the passage in the first box on photocopiable page 139, and to discuss it. Using the rocks in Sample A, they should try Experiment 1, which is described below the box on photocopiable page 139. Children try to name the rocks, and categorise them according to hardness.

Afterwards, using the rocks in Sample B, children should try to identify which stones came from the beach. In their groups, they should discuss how they could tell (Experiment 2).

Working as a whole class, read and discuss the passage in the second box, about the ways in which cliffs can be worn away.

Afterwards, children should discuss and set up Experiments 3, 4 and 5, as described on photocopiable page 139. Explain to the children that Experiments 4 and 5 have to be left in the deep-freeze until the next day.

In the next session, which should be a day or more after the experiments were set up, discuss the outcome of each experiment with the whole class and link it back to the processes of erosion on coastal areas.

Differentiation

This lesson is accessible to children of all abilities. All the work is undertaken in mixed-ability groups.
● Less able children may benefit from working with human resources (classroom assistants/voluntary helpers), if available.
● More able children could be asked to draw labelled diagrams to illustrate the processes of coastal erosion.

Assessing learning outcomes

Ephemeral evidence
● Observation of, and listening to, the children's discussion while they are sorting and categorising rock types.
● The geographical vocabulary used by the children when undertaking the activities.
● Teamwork and co-operation – how well do the children work together in groups?

Vocabulary
erosion
eroded
waves
wind
hydraulic action
abrasion
notch
solution
freeze/thaw action
saturated rock

**Follow-up
activity**
Children could use
secondary sources
(maps, atlases,
reference books,
the Internet) to
locate different
coastal features,
identify the
underlying rock
types and classify
them according to
hardness.

CHAPTER 3
WATER AND ITS
EFFECTS ON THE
LANDSCAPE

Investigating
coasts

① What are these coastal features called?
hour

Learning objectives
- Ask geographical questions.
- Use appropriate geographical vocabulary.
- Use maps.
- Locate places and environments studied.
- Use secondary sources of information.
- Investigate water and its effects on landscapes and people, including the physical features of coasts, and the processes of erosion and deposition that affect them.
- Recognise some physical processes and explain how these can cause changes in places and environments.

Lesson organisation
Initial teacher-led introduction and brainstorm about coastal features caused by erosion, followed by whole-class discussion and identification of coastal features in photographs. Working in six mixed-ability groups of about five or six, children complete the first part of photocopiable page 140, then, working in pairs, they complete the second part. Finally, children locate examples of features on maps. Whole-class plenary session at the end. Start a collective glossary of terms to put in a class book about coasts.

What you need and preparation
You will need: photographs of coastal features caused by erosion (provided by the teacher, from magazines, calendars etc); a copy of photocopiable page 140 for each child; a copy of photocopiable page 139 per pair, for reference; Ordnance Survey maps of areas showing examples of coastal features; wall map of the UK.

What to do

⑩ Introduction
10 mins
Explain to the children the focus of the lesson:
- to identify and name the landscape features created by the processes of erosion on a coastline
- to use the correct geographical vocabulary when describing the coastline and the agents and processes of erosion
- to label a flow chart of the development of coastal features caused by erosion.

Working with the whole class, introduce the lesson with a brainstorming session by asking the children if they can give any examples of coastlines in the UK that are being eroded (and can locate them on a wall map of the UK), or name any physical features caused by erosion. Discuss the processes involved in the formation of coastal features such as caves, arches and stacks (see 'Background information' on page 61).

㊺ Development
45 mins
As a class, look at the photographs of coastal features caused by erosion, and help the children to identify and name these features.

Working in six mixed-ability groups of five or six children, depending on the size of the class, the children discuss the field sketch of a piece of coastline on photocopiable page 140. Then, working individually, the children label the field sketch using the following words: headland, beach, bay, cave, arch, notch, stack.

Working in pairs, the children re-read the passage in the second, larger box on photocopiable page 139 to remind them of the processes of erosion. Then, in the same pairs, they discuss the sequence of drawings at the bottom of photocopiable page 140 describing the development of a stack. For each drawing, the children should explain to each other what they think has happened and why. Then they should write an appropriate caption for each drawing in the process, and finally label the sketches with the names of the features shown.

Working in mixed-ability groups once again, the children should locate examples of these features on Ordnance Survey maps.

⑤ Plenary
5 mins
At the end of the lesson, children should feed back the information they have learned about coastal features produced by erosion. Start a collective glossary of terms to put in a class book about coasts.

Differentiation
This lesson is accessible to children of all abilities. The work is undertaken in mixed-ability groups.

Less able children may benefit from working with human resources (classroom assistants/ voluntary helpers), if available. They could also be provided with word lists from which to take the labels for the activity on photocopiable page 140.

More able children may be given a photograph (selected by the teacher) of similar coastal features and asked to draw a labelled sketch diagram.

CHAPTER 3
WATER AND ITS
EFFECTS ON THE
LANDSCAPE

Investigating
coasts

Assessing learning outcomes

Ephemeral evidence

- Observation of, and listening to, the children working on the activities.
- Geographical vocabulary used by the children when undertaking the activities.
- Teamwork and co-operation – how well do the children work together in groups and in pairs?

Retainable evidence

- Completed photocopiable page 140.
- Glossary of terms produced by the class.

Vocabulary

headland
cliff
beach
bay
cave
arch
notch
stack

ICT opportunities

Use the Internet as a source of the most recent information to support the follow-up activity (see below).

Follow-up activity

If possible, children could visit a place on the coast with some of the features they have been studying. They could investigate items in the news, where cliffs are receding, putting homes and hotels at risk of sliding into the sea, or where whole villages have disappeared into the sea. They should discuss and describe the processes that have caused these problems. Children could use the Internet to obtain information.

What is this coastal settlement like?

What you need and preparation

This lesson plan can be used twice, investigating coastal settlements in the UK in one lesson, and in Europe in the next. Alternatively, if time is a problem, the UK and European investigations can be run simultaneously, as described below. The places named here are only suggestions – you may wish to select other coastal settlements for very valid geographical reasons. Think about the resources you have available for the children to undertake independent research; for example, access to the Internet, number and quality of up-to-date reference books, maps, photographs, photopacks, and so on. If resources are a concern, your local library may be able to help. Also, for European coastal settlements, it might be useful to approach the embassies of the countries concerned (remember to state exactly what information you require). For coastal settlements in the UK, the Tourist Information Centre of the town should be able to send materials.

You will need: a copy of photocopiable page 141 for each child; access to the Internet; maps of the UK and Europe; photographs of the different coastal settlements; reference books.

What to do

10 mins Introduction

Explain to the children the focus of the lesson:
- to identify and describe what places are like and where they are located
- to carry out research about coastal settlements, and communicate the findings
- to investigate the functions of coastal settlements and how they relate to the physical features of the coastline
- to investigate how settlements differ and change, including why they differ in size and character

Learning objectives

- Ask geographical questions.
- Use appropriate geographical vocabulary.
- Collect and record evidence.
- Communicate in ways appropriate to the task and audience.
- Use secondary sources of information.
- Use ICT to help in geographical investigations.
- Learn about similarities and differences between places.
- Identify and describe what places are like.
- Locate the places and environments studied.
- Investigate water and its effects on landscapes and people.
- Investigate how settlements differ and change.

Lesson organisation

Initial teacher introduction; brainstorm of the uses of coastal areas; children find out which European countries have no coastline. In eight mixed-ability groups of four or five, children locate named coastal settlements in the UK and Europe; this is followed by a group research activity and a plenary session to feed back to the whole class.

Investigating coasts

Vocabulary
physical and
human features
coastal
settlements
facilities
function
environmental
concerns

Introduce the lesson by asking the whole class to brainstorm uses of different coastal areas both in the UK and in Europe. For example, people use the coast for fishing, ship-building, as ports for bringing in foreign goods, for tourism and leisure, and so on.

Ask the children, in pairs, to use a map to find and list the European countries that have no coastline.

50 mins Development
Working in mixed-ability groups of about four, the children should locate the following places on a map of the UK: Plymouth, Llandudno, Aberdeen, Holyhead, Grimsby and Torquay. (These are only suggestions – you may wish to select other coastal settlements.)

Next, ask the children to locate the following places on a map of Europe: Majorca, Calais, Rotterdam, Benidorm. (Again, these are only suggestions.)

Now, still working in mixed-ability groups, children use the Internet and other reference sources to research one of the locations named above. They should aim to answer questions such as:
● What is the main economic activity on which the settlement focuses?
● How does the physical landscape make this place good for this kind of activity?
● How has the place changed over time?
Children can use photocopiable page 141 to make notes and to help focus their research.

15 mins Plenary
At the end of the lesson, ask each group of children to feed back what they have found out to the class. How are the places studied similar and how are they different?

Differentiation
This lesson is accessible to children of all abilities; the work is undertaken in mixed-ability groups.

Less able children may benefit from working with human resources (classroom assistants/voluntary helpers), if available. Photocopiable page 141 could be adapted so that it is more accessible to less able children. Reference material should also be provided at an easier level.

More able children could undertake a comparative study, in pairs, of a coastal settlement in the UK with a similar one in Europe (for example, they could compare and contrast a port in the UK with a port in Europe).

Assessing learning outcomes
Ephemeral evidence
● Observation of, and listening to, the children as they undertake the research.
● Responses to the teacher's questioning.
● Geographical vocabulary used by the children when undertaking the activity.
● Teamwork and co-operation – how well do the children work together in groups and in pairs?
Retainable evidence
● Children's completed photocopiable page 141.

ICT opportunities
Children should use the Internet and CD-ROMs (among other reference sources) to research coastal locations.

Follow-up activity
Children could use the information collected to make a class book on coastal settlements in the UK and Europe.

CHAPTER 3
WATER AND ITS
EFFECTS ON THE
LANDSCAPE

Investigating
coasts

 # Where do people go on holiday?

What you need and preparation

You will need: tourist brochures for UK seaside holidays and specialist holidays (for example, birdwatching); access to the Internet; atlases, maps and other reference books; access to computers with word-processing or DTP software; photocopiable page 142 copied on to card, with the twelve 'client profile' cards cut out (one card for each group); twelve photocopies of the class holiday brochure (one for each group) once complete; photocopiable page 143 copied on to card, with the twelve 'Holiday-maker' role-play cards cut out (one card for each group).

What to do

10 mins Introduction

Introduce the lesson with a discussion about UK seaside holidays. The UK has a rich variety of coastal environments – sandy beaches and bays, rocky coasts, cliffs, sand dunes, mud flats and so on. People visit coastal areas at different times of the year and for different reasons.

Explain to the children that in this lesson the class is taking on the role of a travel company and that they are going to produce a class holiday brochure illustrating different holiday destinations in the UK for people who require different types of coastal holidays. The company has done some market research and has found out that they have twelve different types of client to cater for, as characterised on the 'client profile' cards on photocopiable page 142.

Explain to the children the focus of the lesson:
* to find out about different coastal resorts and the features and facilities they offer
* to produce a class holiday brochure, describing and illustrating different resorts
* to use the information in the brochure to decide on suitable holidays for people with different needs.

55 mins Development

Divide the class into twelve groups of two or three children, depending on the size of the class. Allocate each group a different type of prospective client – give them one of the 'client profile' cards from photocopiable page 142. Ask the children to plan a week's holiday for the type of client they are given. Using the Internet, maps and reference books, the children should locate a suitable place in the UK to satisfy their clients. They should describe (using the persuasive genre) and illustrate their holiday destination, which will be combined with those from the other groups to make a class holiday brochure. Each group should produce one page on their destination, using word-processing or DTP software if possible. When the groups have completed their contributions, collect the pages and combine them into the class holiday brochure. Make twelve photocopies of the brochure to be used in the next part of the activity.

Give each group a 'Holiday-maker' card from photocopiable page 143. Ask the children to read their card and, in role, to select a holiday from the class brochure. The group must be prepared to state, in role, why they have chosen that holiday.

10 mins Plenary

Each group should feed back to the class, in role, explaining their choice of holiday and the reasons for it.

Investigating coasts

ICT opportunities
Children should use the Internet to obtain the most recent information about holiday destinations, and could use word-processing or DTP packages to present their holiday brochure pages.

Follow-up activity
Ask the children to select a holiday from the class holiday brochure that they personally would like to go on, and to give reasons for their choice.

Differentiation

This lesson is accessible to children of all abilities. The work is undertaken in mixed-ability groups.

Less able children may benefit from working with human resources (classroom assistants/voluntary helpers), if available. Less able children may be provided with a writing frame to support them when writing the page for the class holiday brochure.

More able children can work at their own appropriate level, since the activity is open-ended.

Assessing learning outcomes

Ephemeral evidence

● Observation of, and listening to, the children as they work on their brochure pages.
● Geographical vocabulary used by the children when undertaking the activity.

Retainable evidence

● Pages for the class holiday brochure.

Settlements

Introduction

The Programme of Study for children at Key Stage 2 (National Curriculum for Geography, 2000), in its Breadth of Study section, makes specific reference to the teaching of knowledge, skills and understanding through the study of two localities and three themes (see 'What is geography?' on page 3). This chapter is designed to address one of those themes in particular: 'How settlements differ and change, including why they differ in size and character, and an issue arising from changes in land-use' (6d).

Within this theme various strands can be identified:
- how and why settlements are different in size and character
- how and why settlements change over time
- issues arising from changes in land use — how the changes affect local communities and environments, for example.

All of these strands are addressed within and across the two units in this chapter, 'Investigating settlements' and 'Using TV to support the study of settlements'. These units cover similar skills and ideas, but do so using different types of resources and secondary sources of evidence.

'Investigating settlements' is largely based on paper sources, current and historical maps and photographs, whilst 'Using TV to support the study of settlements' explains how a television series can be used as the focus for geographical investigations. This is a particularly useful approach for many primary schools, as visiting a range of settlements may not be a realistic possibility.

The four aspects of geography, as specified in the National Curriculum (2000) Programme of Study, can be taught through the settlements theme:
- **Geographical enquiry and skills** – for example, children use secondary sources to identify evidence of change in settlements.
- **Knowledge and understanding of places** – for example, children develop a framework of locational knowledge through study of different places and settlements.
- **Knowledge and understanding of patterns and processes** – for example, children develop ideas about settlement types and patterns, such as the common features of defensive sites, or of ports.
- **Knowledge and understanding of environmental change and sustainable development** – for example, children begin to understand the impact of industry in settlements, and on the environment.

Investigating settlements

Background information

A settlement contains homes, and homes contain people, so we often call settlements communities. Looking at communities means looking at the lives of the people living in them.

A settlement is a place where people live and sometimes work. Most settlements are permanent, and people have lived in these places for hundreds of years.

The site of a settlement is concerned with the key characteristics of where a settlement is located; for example, on a river, on a hill or on the coast.

The situation of a settlement is concerned with where the settlement is located in relation to the rest of the area, county, region, country and so on.

The function of a settlement is the main purpose or reason for the settlement being there today, or in the past. Some settlements have special functions because of what happens or has happened in them. The function of a settlement links its character and situation with the economic activities that go on there. For example, if an industrial town's main function is manufacturing goods, its situation may be due to proximity to raw materials (say, coal), or access to water for power or cooling. A settlement's function may change over time and for many different reasons.

Another aspect of function is the different services and facilities that settlements provide. For example, in a small hamlet there are houses to live in, but no shops or other services, while in a large town there are a wide range of shops, leisure services and so on (see 'Background information' for 'Contrasting localities' on page 19 for an explanation of the settlement hierarchy).

Generally, the shape of a settlement can be described in one of three ways: linear, where most buildings in the settlement follow a line (for example, in a steep-sided valley); nucleated, where most buildings are clustered around a point (for example, in an urban area); and dispersed, where most buildings are spread out (for example, a farming settlement). The shape and layout of any settlement is closely related to the main land-uses and function of that place. For example, a seaside resort will characteristically follow the coastline, and land-uses will relate to the accommodation and entertainment of tourists.

When exploring different types of settlements, there are certain key questions that need to be considered, as listed below:

● What are the origins of the settlement? Are there any clues about the age of the settlement? Place names help us find out something about the origin of settlements. For example, Chester (Roman city and fortified settlement) and Bideford (Anglo-Saxon name, meaning 'ford over river').

● What is the site of the settlement? Is it by a river, on a hill, by the sea?

● What is the situation of the settlement? Where is the settlement in relation to other places?

● What is the size of the settlement in terms of population and area?

● What is the layout of the settlement like? Is it a compact (nucleated) settlement or is it spread out (dispersed)? Is the settlement distributed along a main road or a railway line, for example?

● What are the main land-uses in this settlement – farming, industry, housing, commerce?

● What is the function of this settlement? What facilities does it have – houses, shops, industrial areas, hospital, market square, town hall, leisure facilities, remains of a castle, cattle market?

● What things can you do here – live, work, go out for a meal, go shopping, go to the theatre?

● Is there a dominant feature? For example, does industry dominate the settlement?

● What transport links are there? Where can you get to, and how? What forms of transport does this settlement have?

● How is this settlement changing? What is happening in the settlement and why?

● What type of settlement is this – individual dwelling, hamlet, village, town, city, conurbation?

● Where is this place in this hierarchy of settlements? What are the reasons for this?

● Who does this settlement serve – just those living or working within the settlement, or people in surrounding areas too?

UNIT: Investigating Settlements

Enquiry questions	Teaching objectives	Teaching activities	Learning outcomes	Cross-curricular links
Where are these settlements located? How do we locate places on maps? How do we use indexes and contents pages in an atlas? What do map symbols mean? How do we use scale? How do we use grid references to find settlements?	● Locate places and environments studied. ● Use maps and secondary sources of information. ● Use appropriate geographical vocabulary. ● Recognise how places fit within the wider geographical context and are interdependent.	These ideas could form an introductory session to the rest of the unit: teacher could lead a discussion on how to use an atlas. Children could locate the British Isles and the countries therein, the capital cities of the countries, and their own locality, plus an isolated dwelling, a hamlet, a village, a town and a city (near to where the children live if possible); Children name the county in which they live. When locating settlements, children use the key, compass directions and scale. Children use 4- or 6-figure grid references to locate features; Teacher could then lead a discussion on how these settlements are interconnected and interdependent.	Children: ● can use the contents list and index of an atlas. ● can use grid references to locate settlements.	Numeracy: grid references, scale
What different types of settlement are there? What types of settlement are in our region? How and why are some settlements similar and different to others? How do places fit within the wider geographical context and how are they interdependent?	● Locate places and environments studied. ● Use appropriate geographical vocabulary. ● Collect and record evidence. ● Analyse evidence and draw conclusions. ● Identify and describe what places are like. ● Explain why places are like they are. ● Describe and explain how and why places are similar to and different from others. ● Recognise how places fit in the wider geographical context and are interdependent. ● Recognise and explain patterns made by physical and human environmental features.	Children use atlases and maps to locate the British Isles and the countries therein, the capital cities, and their own locality. They locate an isolated dwelling, a hamlet, a village, a town and a city in their home region, chosen by the teacher. When using the maps, children use the key, compass directions and scale, and use 4- or 6-figure grid references to locate features; In groups, children use maps, photographs, secondary sources of information and first hand experience to review the features associated with each type of settlement (isolated dwelling, hamlet, village, town, city), indicating why the settlement is categorised as it is; They use photocopiable page 144 to record their findings; Each group reports back to the class.	● can use the contents and index of an atlas. ● can use grid references to locate settlements. ● can identify the different features and land-uses of a settlement.	
Why is this settlement here? What does the site, situation and function of a settlement mean? What are some key characteristics and functions of settlements?	● Use maps. ● Use secondary sources of information. ● Locate places and environments studied. ● Use appropriate geographical vocabulary. ● Ask geographical questions. ● Describe and explain how and why places are similar to and different from other places. ● Recognise and explain patterns made by individual physical and human features in the environment.	Children discuss what is meant by the 'situation', 'site' and 'function' of a settlement; In groups, children discuss the site and situation of their own settlement and feed this back to the whole class; Working in groups, children write a brief description of the site and situation of each of the settlements studied in the previous lesson; Working in pairs, children complete photocopiable page 145 by locating and naming two examples of settlements with key site characteristics and functions.	● are able to discuss the site and situation of their own settlement. ● can recognise and describe the site and situation of other settlements.	Literacy: writing lists
What happens in this settlement? What economic activities take place in these settlements?	● Use maps. ● Use secondary sources of information. ● Locate places and environments studied. ● Use appropriate geographical vocabulary. ● Ask geographical questions. ● Describe and explain how and why places are similar to and different from others. ● Recognise and explain patterns made by physical and human environmental features. ● Recognise how places fit in a wider geographical context and are interdependent.	Children discuss what economic activities are, and how they can be described as primary, secondary and tertiary; Using available resources, children list the economic activities found in the isolated dwelling, hamlet, village, town and city studied in the previous two lessons; Using these lists, children highlight relevant activities on photocopiable page 146 for each settlement; Each group reports back to the class; Children compare economic activities and services in the settlements, and look for the hierarchy in services provided; Children select, locate and research one economic activity in one settlement, and present their findings.	● recognise the different types of economic activities in a settlement.	Literacy: discussion genre
How are towns and villages different? What amenities are there in a village and in a town? How do towns and villages differ in terms of services offered? What are the pros and cons of living in a village or a town?	● Investigate how settlements differ and change, including why they differ in size and character. ● Identify and describe what settlements are like. ● Explain why places are like they are. ● Describe and explain how and why places are similar to and different from others. ● Recognise how places fit within the wider geographical context and are interdependent. ● Use the correct geographical vocabulary.	Using photocopiable page 147, which shows the amenities found in a village and in a town, children list the good and bad aspects about living in a village, and living in a town; They write a report about the pros and cons of either living in a village or living in a town, using the discussion genre.	● recognise the different amenities available in a town and in a village. ● discuss the advantages and disadvantages of living in a village and a town.	Literacy: report genre
What is the history of this settlement? How do place names help us find out about the origins of settlements? What other evidence can we use to find out how settlements have changed over time?	● Use the correct geographical vocabulary. ● Locate places and environments studied. ● Use secondary sources of information. ● Collect and record evidence. ● Analyse evidence and draw conclusions. ● Explain why places are like they are. ● Investigate how settlements differ and change, including why they differ in size and character. ● Recognise and explain patterns made by human features in the environment.	Teacher leads a discussion about how place names help us find out about the origins of settlements; Using photocopiable page 148, children undertake a place name survey of the local area. Then, they undertake a similar survey of another area of the UK (eg a contrasting locality, or one that children have visited, or that links with another curriculum area); Children use historical evidence (e.g. old maps and photographs, old census returns) to study changes in function of their own settlement over time. Each child writes a report on changes in their settlement.	● undertake a 'place name' survey. ● use historical evidence to work out the origins of settlements.	History: use of historical evidence such as maps and census data

Resources
Maps at a range of scales; atlases; old and modern photographs of children's own settlement, including aerial and ground photographs; old maps of own settlement showing historical land-use; other historical documents relating to economic activities and population of own settlement through history; secondary sources of information about the features and functions of different types of settlement being studied – isolated dwelling, hamlet, village, town and city, preferably in local region; highlighter pens for children to use; access to computers with word-processing, spreadsheet and graphics software; access to the Internet; reference books; *Settlements* CD-ROM (Acorn/MAC/PC) from Anglia Multimedia; copies of photocopiable page 144–148.

Investigating
settlements

① hour What different types of settlements are there?

Learning objectives
- Use maps and secondary sources of information.
- Locate places and environments studied.
- Use appropriate geographical vocabulary.
- Ask geographical questions.
- Collect and record evidence.
- Analyse evidence and draw conclusions.
- Identify and describe what places are like.
- Explain why places are like they are.
- Describe and explain how and why places are similar to and different from other places.
- Recognise how places fit within the wider geographical context and are interdependent.
- Recognise and explain patterns made by individual physical and human features in the environment.

Lesson organisation
Initial teacher-led introduction and discussion with whole class, followed by enquiry activity about features of different types of settlement, carried out by children in six mixed-ability groups of five to six. Whole-class plenary session at the end.

Vocabulary
settlements
isolated dwelling
villages
town
city
conurbation
services
market town
industrial estates
crossing point of a river
harbour
port
rural
urban
hamlet

What you need and preparation
Select an isolated dwelling, a hamlet, village, town and city for children to study in this and the following lessons. Choose settlements for which resources are readily available (photographs, maps, reference books and so on), and which are in the local area, if possible.

You will need: maps of the area being studied, at a range of scales; aerial photographs of the settlements, if available; secondary sources of evidence (for example, reference books, ground-level photographs) about the settlements being investigated; access to the Internet; *Settlements* CD-ROM (Anglia Multimedia); copies of photocopiable page 144 (enough for each group to have one sheet per settlement type); highlighter pens.

What to do

⑩ mins Introduction
Using atlases and maps, children locate the United Kingdom and the countries therein, the capital cities of the countries, and their own locality. Then help them to locate a particular isolated dwelling, hamlet, village, town and city in their locality. These will be the settlements studied in this and the following lessons.

When locating settlements using maps, children should practise using the key, compass directions and scale. They should use four- or six-figure grid references to locate the settlements.

The teacher could lead a short discussion on how these settlements are interconnected and interdependent.

Explain to the children the focus of the lesson:
- to use atlases and maps to locate the local region, and locate settlements of different types
- to investigate how and why settlements differ in size and character
- to use maps, photographs and other sources of information to learn about the different features of the settlements
- to ask geographical questions about the sites, situations and functions of the different settlements
- to see how places fit within the wider geographical context and are interdependent.

Through questioning, find out what the children already know about settlements in general and the settlements being investigated in particular.

㊵ mins Development
Ask the children, working in mixed-ability groups, to review the features associated with each type of settlement – isolated dwelling, hamlet, village, town and city – using maps, photographs, secondary sources of information (including the Internet and CD-ROMs), and first-hand experience (assuming the settlements are in the local region). They should record their findings by highlighting the relevant words and descriptions on photocopiable page 144 (one copy for each settlement). Once the children have completed a review of each settlement, ask them to say what type of settlement it is, and to explain why it is categorised as this.

⑩ mins Plenary
At the end of the lesson, the groups feed back information they have found out about each settlement to the rest of the class.

Differentiation

● Less able children could be provided with an easier version of photocopiable page 144, and simpler maps of the settlements than Ordnance Survey maps. Ask them to use co-ordinates instead of grid references to locate the places. Use human resources (classroom assistants/voluntary helpers), if available, to work with less able children.

● More able children could locate similar settlements in other areas using four- or six-figure grid references, as appropriate to the abilities of the children.

Assessing learning outcomes

Ephemeral evidence

● Observation of, and listening to, the children's discussion as they carry out the activity.

● Questions asked by the children and answers given to questions framed by the teacher.

● Geographical vocabulary used by the children when undertaking the activity.

● Teamwork and co-operation – how well do the children work together in groups?

Retainable evidence

● Children's completed copies of photocopiable page 144.

ICT opportunities
Children could use the Internet to research information about the settlements. (See also 'Follow-up activity', below.)

Follow-up activity
Children could use the *Settlements* CD-ROM from Anglia Multimedia to find out about different types of settlements. Ask the children to click on a type of settlement (for example, an English village, conurbation or market town) and they will then see a list from which they can choose a particular feature. Ask them to click on a chosen theme or feature; they will find photographic images, maps and some informative text.

① Why is this settlement here?
(1 hour)

What you need and preparation

You will need: atlases; maps of the local region at a range of scales, including Ordnance Survey maps (1:50 000); aerial photographs and other secondary sources of information about the site, situation and function of the children's own settlement; sources of information about the site and situation of each of the settlements studied in the previous lesson ('What different types of settlements are there?'); a copy of photocopiable page 145 for each child.

What to do

⑩ Introduction
(10 mins)

Introduce the lesson to the whole class by recapping geographical vocabulary describing settlements. Discuss with the children what we mean by the 'situation', 'site' and 'function' of a settlement (see 'Background information' on page 72).

Explain to the children the focus of the lesson:

● to learn about the site, situation and function of different settlements, especially the children's own settlement

● to investigate how and why settlements differ in size and character, and in situation and function

● to use maps and other sources of information to locate settlements with certain key characteristics of site and function

● to use the correct geographical vocabulary when talking about settlements.

㊺ Development
(45 mins)

Working in six mixed-ability groups of five or six children, depending on the size of the class, children should use maps, aerial photographs and other secondary resources to find out about and discuss the site and situation of their own settlement. After ten

Learning objectives
● Use maps.
● Use secondary sources of information.
● Locate places and environments studied.
● Use appropriate geographical vocabulary.
● Ask geographical questions.
● Describe and explain how and why places are similar to and different from other places.
● Recognise and explain patterns made by individual physical and human features in the environment.

Lesson organisation
Initial teacher-led discussion with whole-class recapping geographical vocabulary used to describe settlements. Then, two enquiry activities on the site, situation and function of the children's own settlement, and of the settlements studied in the previous lesson. For these activities, children work in six mixed-ability groups of five or six, then move on to pair work using photocopiable page 145, and a whole-class plenary session at the end.

Vocabulary
site
situation
function
market town
seaside resort
fishing port
ferry port
harbour
industrial centre
administration
centre
defensive sites
bridging points
wet-point sites

**ICT
opportunities**
Children could use
the Internet to find
additional
information about
the key
characteristics of
the settlements
identified on
photocopiable page
145. (See also
'Follow-up activity',
below.)

**Follow-up
activity**
Children could use
the *Settlements*
CD-ROM from
Anglia Multimedia
to find out about
settlements with
different sites and
different functions.
They could
compare and
contrast these
different
settlements.

minutes or so, they should feed back to the whole class.

Working in the same groups, the children then write a brief description of the site and situation of each of the settlements studied in the previous lesson ('What different types of settlements are there?', page 74), using maps and secondary sources. They should include information on the relative positions of the settlements, and compass directions and distances from their own settlement. On completion, groups should feed back to the whole class, each group reading out its description of one of the settlements.

Then, working in pairs and using maps at different scales, the children complete photocopiable page 145. This involves locating and naming examples of settlements that have the key characteristics and functions described.

(5 mins) Plenary
At the end of the lesson, the children discuss as a class what they have found out about the sites, situations and functions of settlements.

Differentiation

Less able children could be provided with lists of vocabulary (word banks) to help them to complete photocopiable page 145. Use some of the words listed in the 'Vocabulary' list for this lesson (above), as appropriate to the ability level of the children, and also words specific to their own settlement. Less able children could also be supplied with a simplified version of photocopiable page 145 and with simpler maps than Ordnance Survey maps. Use human resources (classroom assistants/voluntary helpers), if available, to work with less able children.

More able children could take one of the settlements they have identified as having a key characteristic of site or function (on photocopiable page 145) and find out more about it, using secondary sources, reference materials and the Internet, if appropriate.

Assessing learning outcomes
Ephemeral evidence
● Observation of, and listening to, the children's discussion as they carry out the activity.
● Questions asked by the children and answers given to questions framed by the teacher.
● Geographical vocabulary used by the children when undertaking the activity.
● Teamwork and co-operation – how well do the children work together in groups?
Retainable evidence
● Written descriptions of the site and situation of each of the settlements.
● Children's completed photocopiable page 145.

What happens in this settlement?

What you need and preparation

You will need: atlases; maps at a range of scales; aerial and ground-level photographs of different settlements and different economic activities; other secondary sources, such as reference books; access to the Internet; access to computers with spreadsheet software; copies of photocopiable page 146 (enough for each child to have one copy for each settlement); highlighter pens.

What to do

15 mins Introduction

Explain to the children the focus of the lesson:

● to learn about the economic functions of settlements

● to use maps and secondary sources of information to locate and find out about settlements with different economic functions

● to appreciate that jobs provide money for people to spend, which in turn provides jobs for others

● to see how places fit within the wider geographical context and are interdependent

● to use the correct geographical vocabulary when talking about settlements.

Introduce the lesson to the whole class by discussing what economic activities are and how these activities can be described as 'primary' (taking raw resources from the Earth), 'secondary' (making and manufacturing goods) and 'tertiary' (services selling to and serving the communities) economic activities. (See 'Background information' on page 72.)

40 mins Development

The whole class should work together to brainstorm and list the economic activities found in the isolated dwelling, hamlet, village, town and city studied in the previous two lessons ('What different types of settlements are there?' and 'Why is this settlement here?', pages 74 and 75). Use photographs and other reference materials to help supplement the brainstormed list.

Working in six mixed-ability groups of five or six, and using the lists created in the brainstorming session, ask the children to highlight and complete a copy of photocopiable page 146 for each of the settlements. Children should compare the economic activities found in the different settlement types, and discuss how the settlements differ in terms of the services provided. Ask the children if they can see a hierarchy in the services provided. Ask the groups to report back to the rest of the class on their findings.

Working in the same groups, the children now select, locate and research (using the Internet, if appropriate) one economic activity and a settlement in which this economic activity is the focus.

Ask the children to present their findings to the rest of the class. Compare the economic activities found in the different settlement types covered by the groups.

5 mins Plenary

At the end of the lesson, discuss with the children as a whole class which economic activity they would like to be involved in and why.

Differentiation

Less able children could be provided with a simplified version of photocopiable page 146, and with

---

Learning objectives
● Use maps.
● Use secondary information sources.
● Locate places and environments studied.
● Use appropriate geographical vocabulary.
● Ask geographical questions.
● Describe and explain how and why places are similar to and different from other places.
● Recognise and explain patterns made by individual physical and human features in the environment.
● Recognise how places fit within a wider geographical context and are interdependent.

Lesson organisation
Whole-class introduction to discuss what economic activities are and how they can be divided into 'primary', 'secondary' and 'tertiary'. Whole-class brainstorm to list economic activities, followed by group work: children work in six mixed-ability groups of five or six, using the lists to complete photocopiable page 146. Group work to locate one economic activity and a settlement in which this activity is the focus, and then to present their findings to the class; whole-class plenary at the end.

Vocabulary
primary economic activities
secondary economic activities
tertiary economic activities
agriculture
mixed farming
arable farming
dairy farming
horticulture
mining
manufacturing
industries
services
medical services
emergency services
education
financial and legal services
leisure facilities

Follow-up activities
● For each of the settlements, children could produce a spreadsheet on the computer to help record and analyse the data recorded for each settlement using photocopiable page 146. They could use the spreadsheet to make comparisons between settlements.
● Children could write up descriptions of the economic activities found in each settlement, using word-processing software.

simpler maps than Ordnance Survey maps. Use human resources (classroom assistants/voluntary helpers), if available, to work with less able children.

More able children could locate and research (using the Internet if appropriate) a second, contrasting economic activity and a settlement in which this economic activity is the focus, seeing how the different activity affects the character and features of the settlement as compared with that studied in the main part of the lesson.

Assessing learning outcomes
Ephemeral evidence
● Observation of, and listening to, the children's discussion as they carry out the activities.
● Questions asked by the children and answers given to questions framed by the teacher.
● Geographical vocabulary used by the children when undertaking the activities.
● Teamwork and co-operation – how well do the children work together in groups?
Retainable evidence
● Children's completed copies of photocopiable page 146.

How are towns and villages different?
(1 hour)

Learning objectives
● Investigate how settlements differ and change, including why they differ in size and character.
● Identify and describe what settlements are like.
● Explain why places are like they are.
● Describe and explain how and why places are similar to and different from other places.
● Recognise how places fit within the wider geographical context and are interdependent.
● Use the correct geographical vocabulary.
● Ask geographical questions.

Lesson organisation
Initial teacher-led introduction and discussion with whole class, followed by enquiry activity using the information provided on photocopiable page 147 and knowledge learned in the previous lessons in this unit. Children work in six mixed-ability groups of five or six, then work individually to produce a report; whole-class plenary session at the end.

What you need and preparation
You will need: a copy of photocopiable page 147 for each child; access to computers with word-processing software.

What to do
(5 mins) Introduction
Introduce the lesson to the whole class by recapping on what has been learned from the lessons so far in this unit about settlements and how they vary in size, character and function.

Explain to the children the focus of the lesson:
● to find out how towns and villages differ in the amenities they offer
● to think about what it's like to live in a town
● to think about what it's like to live in a village
● to write a report on the good and bad things about living in either settlement
● use the correct geographical vocabulary when talking about settlements.

(50 mins) Development
Working in six mixed-ability groups of approximately five or six children (depending on the size of the class), the children should look at the tables of information on photocopiable page 147, which show the amenities found in a village and those located in a town. In their groups the children should:
● list the good and bad aspects of living in a village
● list the good and bad aspects of living in a town.

Working individually, the children should then write a report about the pros (positive benefits) and cons (negative aspects) of either living in a village or living in a town. The report should be written in the discussion genre and may be produced using a word-processing package on the computer. (Children could plan their reports by hand, and then take turns to use the computer, if necessary.)

5 mins Plenary

At the end of the lesson, groups feed back information they have found out about each settlement to the rest of the class.

Differentiation

Less able children could be provided with a discussion genre writing frame and a word bank of useful vocabulary to support them in writing their report. Use human resources (classroom assistants/voluntary helpers), if available, to work with less able children.

More able children could write a letter to the local council, trying to persuade them to encourage people to live in the centre of town, since the regeneration of town centres as living and working communities is high on the political agenda. They should use the persuasive genre of writing. Children could e-mail their letters to the members of the local council, as well as sending printed copies.

Assessing learning outcomes

Ephemeral evidence

- Observation of, and listening to, the children's discussion as they carry out the activities.
- Questions asked by the children and answers given to questions framed by the teacher.
- Geographical vocabulary used by the children when undertaking the activities.
- Teamwork and co-operation – how well do the children work together in groups?

Retainable evidence

- Children's lists of good and bad aspects of living in a village.
- Children's lists of good and bad aspects of living in a town.
- Children's reports about the pros and cons of either living in a village or living in a town.

Vocabulary
settlements
village
town
services
transport
emergency services

ICT opportunities
Children can use word-processing software to write their reports about the positive and negative aspects of living in a town or a village. (See also Follow-up activities, below.)

Follow-up activities
Children could draw posters to show the merits of living in either a village or a town. This poster could be produced using a graphics software package on the computer, if available.

⏱ 1 hour 15 mins What is the history of this settlement?

What you need and preparation

You will need: atlases; Ordnance Survey maps at a range of scales and as appropriate to the area under study; historical evidence (including old maps and historical evidence, which can be sourced from the local Records Office and local libraries); copies of photocopiable page 148 (one for each child).

What to do

55 mins Introduction

Discuss with the children their own surnames and how some of them link to their family in the past. Discuss place names and their origins. Introduce the children to photocopiable page 148 and explain that this is to be their reference to help them interpret settlement names and so find out about the origins of some settlements.

Explain to the children the focus of the lesson:

- to use maps and secondary sources of information, including reference books, historical documents and photographs, to find place names
- to recognise how to use the names of places to study the historical development of settlements and to find out who influenced that development

Learning objectives
- Ask geographical questions.
- Use the correct geographical vocabulary.
- Use maps.
- Locate places and environments studied.
- Use secondary sources of information.
- Collect and record evidence.
- Analyse evidence and draw conclusions.
- Identify and describe what places are like.
- Explain why places are like they are.
- Investigate how settlements differ and change, including why they differ in size and character.
- Recognise and explain patterns made by human features in the environment.
- Describe and explain how and why places are similar to and different from other places.

Lesson organisation
Initial teacher-led introduction and discussion with whole class, followed by enquiry activity in which children work in six mixed-ability groups of five or six to carry out a place name survey of their own area. Afterwards they do a place name survey of another area of the UK. In groups, children then use historical evidence to study changes in function of their own settlement, and work individually to write reports; whole-class plenary session at the end.

Investigating settlements

● to identify, locate and describe what settlements are like and explain why they are like they are
● to use the correct geographical vocabulary when talking about settlements.

10 mins **Development**
Working in mixed-ability groups, using photocopiable page 148, maps and other secondary sources, the children should conduct a place name survey of their own area. They could draw out a table such as the one below, and list the names of places under the appropriate headings:

Celtic (before 400 AD)	Scandinavian (Danes and Norse 800–1100 AD)	Roman (43–450 AD)	Anglo-Saxon (450–1100 AD)

What does the survey tell the children about their area and when it was first settled? Who were the main settlers?

Working in the same groups the children should conduct a place name survey of another area of the UK – perhaps one that the children visit regularly, a contrasting locality, or an area that forms part of a study of another curriculum area (for example, York or Chester have Roman origins, which could be linked with history).

Working in groups, the children should use the historical evidence available (old maps, information from the local Records Office, reference books) to study changes in function that have occurred in their own settlement. They could compare old and new photographs, analyse old maps and examine census returns (all located and borrowed from the local Records Office, local libraries, or local history societies). Working individually, the children then write a report about the changes in their own settlement through history.

10 mins **Plenary**
At the end of the lesson, the groups should feed back the information they have found out about their own settlement and how it has changed over the years. Discuss whether the children feel these changes have been for the better or not.

Differentiation
Less able children could be provided with a writing frame and a word bank of useful vocabulary to support them in writing their report. Use human resources (classroom assistants/voluntary helpers), if available, to work with less able children.

More able children could give the grid references of the places they have named and located for the first activity, naming places in their own area. As a group, the children could look at place names throughout the country. Can they find places that have been influenced more by people in one period of history than another? Ask the children to map their findings and discuss the reasons for their conclusions.

Assessing learning outcomes

Ephemeral evidence

● Observation of, and listening to, the children's discussion as they carry out the activities.
● Questions asked by the children and answers given to questions framed by the teacher.
● Geographical vocabulary used by the children when undertaking the activities.
● Teamwork and co-operation – how well do the children work together in groups?

Retainable evidence

● Children's survey of place names in their own area.
● Children's survey of place names in another area of the UK.
● Children's reports on changes in the function of their own settlement.

Using television to support the study of settlements

Using television

A real benefit of using television to support learning is that the change in pace is very attractive to children in school. They also respond well to explanations and descriptions from people other than their regular teachers. However, it is important to remember that an educational viewing style is needed. Appropriate teaching strategies will help to maximise the educational benefits of using television, and possible suggestions include watching with a specific brief in mind; watching selected sections or entire programmes more than once; using sections only or pausing the programme to explain and review sections; reducing the volume to maximise visual impact.

The particular resource suggested for use in the following lesson plans is the BBC *Landmarks* video series entitled *Using the Land* (Video Plus) 2000 published by BBC Worldwide, Educational Publishing, London (ISBN 0 563 46513 1). This pack comprises five video programmes, each of about 20 minutes duration, which look at various settlements in the UK, examining their characters and functions, and the ways in which they have changed through history.

Programme 1 – 'Growing Settlements' looks at Brailes and Solihull

Programme 2 – 'Changing Industry' looks at Barrow and Appleby

Programme 3 – 'Digging the Landscape' looks at Orgreave and Blue Circle Quarry

Programme 4 – 'Coastal Neighbours' looks at Tenby and Milford Haven

Programme 5 – 'Redeveloping the Inner City' looks at Sheffield and Bradford.

Brief details about the settlements are given in 'Background information', below. The resource also includes colour photographs and additional information.

In this unit, two introductory lessons are described, followed by a third lesson that should be repeated five times – once for each programme viewed. In a concluding lesson the children then draw together what has been learned from the programmes, in the context of their own settlement.

Background information

The settlements featured in the programmes and photographs in the *Using the Land* pack are:.

Brailes is a village in Warwickshire. Traditionally a farming village, this settlement has more recently seen a sharp decline in population and significant changes in types of economic activity.

Solihull, traditionally a village, now represents part of the conurbation of Birmingham. Good transport links led to growth and expansion in commercial and industrial activity here.

Barrow is on the north-west coast of England, within the county of Cumbria. It is a town that developed as a port and ship-building centre from 1871. The development of this industry was largely due to the situation of Walney Island (a sand bar) which helped to protect Barrow from heavy seas. However, recent technological advancements in ship-building machinery have led to a high level of unemployment here.

Appleby is also located in north-east Cumbria and traditionally functioned as a market town. It is now characterised by more of a mixed economy; the closure of its main farming industry (cheese-making) led to a diversification of economic activity in the area.

Tenby is situated on the South Pembrokeshire coast. Originally a fishing port, it now functions as a resort attracting many tourists.

Further along the South Pembrokeshire coastline (in a westerly direction) is **Milford Haven**, traditionally one of the largest fishing ports in the UK. The main industry here today is oil refining and the area is notorious for the disaster of 1996, when the *Sea Empress* spilt approximately 70 000 tonnes of oil into the sea.

Sheffield is a city in the north of England, which developed as an industrial centre in the eighteenth century. Many factories were built on flat areas within the Don Valley which, as the steel industry declined were demolished, leaving brownfield sites for redevelopment.

Bradford is north-west of Sheffield; traditionally the main industry here was weaving. Today, however, there is evidence of a more mixed economy and relatively high levels of unemployment.

UNIT: Using television to support the study of settlements

Enquiry questions	Teaching objectives	Teaching activities	Learning outcomes	Cross-curricular links
What types of settlements are there in our home region? What are these settlements like? How are they different? How are they similar? Where are these settlements in the UK?	● Use appropriate geographical vocabulary. ● Use atlases, globes, maps and plans. ● Use secondary sources of information. ● Learn about UK localities. ● Ask geographical questions. ● Collect and record evidence. ● Analyse evidence and draw conclusions. ● Identify and describe what places are like. ● Describe and explain how and why places are similar to and different from other places. ● Recognise how places fit within the wider geographical context and are interdependent. ● Locate places and environments studied.	Children locate and discuss different settlements in the region around their own settlement, using maps and aerial photographs. They identify main similarities and differences in terms of type, size, shape, land-use and function, and record their findings using photocopiable page 149. In preparation for viewing the television programmes later in the unit, children locate the settlements featured in the programmes on an interactive classroom display map.	Children: ● begin to understand the main similarities and differences between different settlements within the home region. ● can locate the settlements studied on a map.	
What are these settlements like? What do these photographs show about the settlements? What do we want to find out about these settlements?	● Ask geographical questions. ● Use appropriate geographical vocabulary. ● Use secondary sources of information. ● Learn about UK localities. ● Investigate how settlements differ and change.	Using photographs contained in the teacher's pack accompanying the video series, children predict what each place is like, recording their predictions on photocopiable page 150. In groups of four to six, children think of, and agree on, three geographical questions that they hope to answer using evidence from the programmes in the future lessons.	● can make predictions about settlements using secondary sources of information and prior knowledge. ● can identify appropriate geographical questions.	
How and why do settlements change? How and why have these settlements changed? How do these changes affect the job of the town planner? What else do we want to find out about these settlements? What resources will we need? How and why has our settlement changed?	● Ask geographical questions. ● Collect and record evidence. ● Use appropriate geographical vocabulary. ● Use secondary sources of information. ● Use ICT to help in geographical investigations. ● Learn about UK localities. ● Investigate how settlements differ and change. ● Locate places and environments studied.	The teacher explains that after they have watched five television programmes about settlements in the UK, the children are going to write a report for *The Planner's Gazette* describing how and why different settlements change. Using copies of photocopiable page 151, children identify and record relevant evidence of change from each of the five programmes viewed. In mixed-ability groups of four to six, children review their findings. They organise their own enquiry, list the additional sources they will use, and produce their report using word-processing software.	● can use secondary sources of information to identify the nature and extent of change in different settlements. ● begin to understand how and why settlements change. ● can use ICT to communicate their findings appropriately.	Literacy: report genre ICT: word-processing skills
How and why has our settlement changed? How will current changes affect us and future generations?	● Analyse evidence and draw conclusions. ● Use appropriate geographical vocabulary. ● Use ICT to help in geographical investigations. ● Use decision-making skills. ● Learn about UK localities. ● Investigate an environmental issue. ● Recognise how and why people may seek to manage environments sustainably.	Using their own settlement as a context, children review the changes over the last 100 years. They compile questions to ask a local planner, about how and why things have changed. A planner could be invited into school, and questioned by the children on how and why decisions affecting the settlement were made; After the discussion, children should write a letter to the local planning department, outlining how decisions already made have affected their lives, and the impact that future developments may have. They could e-mail the letter to the planning department as an attachment.	● identify relevant geographical questions relating to change in their local area. ● begin to develop an understanding of environmental change and sustainability within the context of their local area.	ICT: communication skills (e-mail, letter writing)

Resources

BBC *Landmarks* video series and teacher's pack entitled *Using the Land* (Video Plus, 2000, BBC Worldwide, ISBN 0 563 46513 1); atlases; maps of the home region, at a range of scales; aerial photographs of the isolated dwelling, hamlet, village, town and city being investigated, if available; secondary sources of evidence (for example, reference books, ground photographs) about the settlements; access to computers with word-processing software; photographs and other sources of information about your own settlement and the way it has changed over the last 100 years, to including historical maps, copies of which may be obtained from a local record office, and contemporary Ordnance Survey maps (1.50 000); television and VCR; photocopiable pages 149–151.

Display

Interactive display including a UK map with the locations of settlements featured in the programmes labelled on it, and annotated with photographs and commentaries about the different types of settlements; children's reports on settlement change for *The Planner's Gazette*.

CHAPTER 4
SETTLEMENTS

Using television to support the study of settlements

① What types of settlements are there in our home region?
(1 hour)

Learning objectives
- Use appropriate geographical vocabulary.
- Use atlases, globes, maps and plans.
- Use secondary sources of information.
- Learn about UK localities.
- Ask geographical questions.
- Collect and record evidence.
- Analyse evidence and draw conclusions.
- Identify and describe what places are like.
- Describe and explain how and why places are similar to and different from other places.
- Recognise how places fit within the wider geographical context and are interdependent.
- Locate places and environments studied.

Lesson organisation
Initial teacher-led discussion with whole class, followed by work in mixed-ability pairs locating and researching settlements of different types in the home region. Whole-class plenary session at the end, during which children are introduced to a class display showing the settlements featured in television programmes to be viewed later in the unit.

Vocabulary
settlement
hamlet
village
town
city
conurbation
settlement
hierarchy
population
linear
nucleated
dispersed
land-use
function

What you need and preparation
Select an isolated dwelling, a hamlet, village, town and city for children to study in this and the following lessons. Choose settlements for which resources are readily available (photographs, maps, reference books and so on), and which are in the local area, if possible).

You will need: atlases; maps of the areas being studied at a range of scales; aerial photographs of the settlements, if available; secondary sources of evidence (for example, reference books, ground-level photographs) about the areas being investigated; class display of a UK map labelled with locations, names and photographs of settlements to be covered within the television programmes viewed later in the unit (see 'What are these settlements like?' on page 86, and 'Background information' on page 82); two or three copies of photocopiable page 149 for each pair (enough to provide a box for each settlement studied).

What to do
⑩ Introduction
(10 mins) Introduce the lesson to the whole class with a brief discussion on settlement hierarchies. Settlements are places where people live, and can be broadly categorised and ranked in order of size and the services and amenities they offer (see 'Background information' in the 'Contrasting localities' unit introduction on page 19). The settlement hierarchy is as follows: isolated dwelling, hamlet, village, town, city, conurbation (urban areas that have merged together).

Ask the children to name nearby settlements they visit often, and to describe what they do there. Discuss the extent of the home region (county boundaries and so on).

Explain to the children the focus of the lesson:
- to locate and compare different types of settlements within the home region
- to develop locational knowledge of the settlements described in the television programmes that are to be viewed later in the unit (see 'What are these settlements like?', page 86).

40 mins Development
In pairs, children use maps of their home region to locate settlements of different types, selected by the teacher. They use aerial photographs and other secondary sources of information to find out about the shape, size and function of each settlement, and then suggest what type of settlement it is (isolated dwelling, hamlet, village, and so on). They identify a question that they would like to research further, to find out more about a specific aspect of the settlement. Children use photocopiable page 149 to record all this work.

10 mins Plenary
Discuss similarities and differences between the identified settlements. These settlements are all quite close by, so we could find out more by going on a visit. How could we find out more about settlements that are a long distance away? Introduce the idea of finding out about settlements across the UK through the medium of television. Show children the class display, showing the locations of the settlements to be featured in the programmes later in the unit. Run through the name and location of each settlement with them, and ask the children to make sure they have visited the display and become familiar with the locations before the next lesson.

Differentiation
Children should work in mixed-ability pairs.

Less able children may need assistance with working out the area of land covered by each settlement, using the scale on the map. Use human resources (classroom assistants/voluntary helpers), if available, to work with less able children.

More able children could locate different settlements with similar features in other areas of the UK, or in other countries, using an atlas, maps and other resources, including the Internet.

Assessing learning outcomes
Ephemeral evidence
- Observation of, and listening to, the children's discussion as they carry out the activities.
- Questions asked by the children and answers given to questions framed by the teacher.
- Geographical vocabulary used by the children when undertaking the activities.
- Teamwork and co-operation – how well do the children work together in pairs?

Retainable evidence
- Children's completed photocopiable page 149.

ICT opportunities
Children could use the Internet to find out more about the settlements in their home region.

Follow-up activity
Children could use secondary sources of information, including reference books and the Internet, to carry out research to answer the questions they identified for each settlement on photocopiable page 149.

(1 hour) What are these settlements like?

What you need and preparation
You will need: photographs of UK settlements from the BBC 'Landmarks' video series and teacher's pack entitled *Using the Land* (BBC Worldwide, ISBN 0 563 46513 1); UK atlases; a copy of photocopiable page 150 for each child.

What to do

(10 mins) Introduction
Introduce the lesson to the whole class by asking the children to locate Brailes, Solihull (Birmingham), Appleby, Barrow, Sheffield, Bradford, Tenby and Milford Haven on the interactive class display map (see previous lesson, 'What types of settlements are there in our home region?', page 84).

Explain to the children the focus of the lesson:
● to predict what each settlement will be like before watching the programmes
● to list questions they would like to investigate during the next few lessons, using the video programmes and other secondary sources.

(40 mins) Development
Working in six mixed-ability groups of four to six, the children use the photographs from the BBC 'Landmarks' video series and teacher's pack entitled *Using the Land*, plus the class display, to complete photocopiable 150. They look at each photograph, and makes notes about what it shows about the town. These notes are their predictions about what each place is like, which they will test when they 'visit' the settlements in the television programmes. Then, in their groups, the children identify and agree upon three questions about these settlements that they would like and answer, using the television programmes and other resources, in the next lessons. These geographical questions are recorded and can be answered using photocopiable page 150.

(10 mins) Plenary
As a class, list the children's questions recorded on photocopiable page 150 under each settlement name, in preparation for the next lesson ('How and why do settlements change?'), when children will be organised into groups to research and answer them.

CHAPTER 4
SETTLEMENTS

Using television
to support the
study of
settlements

Differentiation

This lesson is accessible to children of all abilities. The work is undertaken in mixed-ability groups.

Less able children may benefit from working with human resources (classroom assistants/ voluntary helpers), if available. Less able children could be asked to focus on one or two settlements only, and may be given additional resources and simpler information to help them to make predictions about what they think each settlement is like.

Assessing learning outcomes

Ephemeral evidence

● Observation of, and listening to, the children's discussion as they carry out the activities.

● Questions asked by the children and answers given to questions framed by the teacher.

● Geographical vocabulary used by the children when undertaking the activities.

● Teamwork and co-operation – how well do the children work together in groups?

Retainable evidence

● The children's completed copies of photocopiable page 150.

● The geographical questions the children identify for investigation in future lessons.

ICT opportunities
Please see 'Follow-up activity', below.

Follow-up activity
Children could use the Internet, and other secondary sources of information, to find out more about one of the settlements in the table on photocopiable page 150. They could print off relevant images and text from the Internet and add them to the class display.

③ hours How and why do settlements change?

What you need and preparation

You will need: all five video programmes in the BBC *Landmarks* video series and teacher's pack entitled *Using the Land* (BBC Worldwide, ISBN 0 563 46513 1); copies of the questions generated by children, listed under the name of each settlement from the previous lesson ('What are these settlements like?'); UK atlases; access to computers with word-processing software; two copies of photocopiable 151 for each child per programme (one copy for each settlement).

What to do

⟨20 mins⟩ Introduction

Introduce the lesson to the whole class by reminding the children of the questions they raised about the settlements studied in the previous lesson ('What are these settlements like?'). Give the children copies of photocopiable page 151 to record evidence of change in the settlements featured while watching the television programmes.

Explain to the children the focus of the lesson:

● to identify and record evidence of change in different settlements, using television as a secondary source

● to begin to answer the questions raised about the settlements during the previous lesson

● to write a report on how and why settlements have changed, for 'The Planner's Gazette'.

Learning objectives
● Ask geographical questions.
● Collect and record evidence.
● Use appropriate geographical vocabulary.
● Use secondary sources of information.
● Use ICT to help in geographical investigations.
● Learn about UK localities.
● Investigate how settlements differ and change.
● Locate places and environments studied.

Lesson organisation
Teacher-led introduction with whole class discussing the questions raised about settlements in the previous lesson, and how they are going to answer them using evidence from television programmes. The next part of this lesson is effectively repeated five times over a number of days, as children watch each of the television programmes. For each programme, children make notes about how settlements have changed on a separate copy of photocopiable page 151. Whole-class plenary following each programme to discuss findings; then in six mixed-ability groups of four to six, children prepare a report on change in settlements for 'The Planner's Gazette'.

CHAPTER 4
SETTLEMENTS

Using television to support the study of settlements

bear in mind the specific strategies outlined in 'Background information' on page 82

Vocabulary
settlement
hamlet
village
town
city
conurbation
linear
nucleated
dispersed
land-use
function
farming
commercial
industrial
coast
sand bar
port
market town
economic
activity
tourism
brownfield site
mixed economy

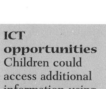 **Development**

Part 1: accessing information from the television programmes (20 minutes each, plus plenary discussion)

Children watch each of the five programmes in the BBC 'Landmarks' video series entitled *Using the Land*. The programmes can be watched on separate occasions over a number of days. While the children are watching, bear in mind the specific strategies outlined in 'Background information' on page 82 for maximising the teaching value of the experience. The children should concentrate on how various aspects of the settlements featured in the programmes have changed over time – for example, jobs, shops, housing and land-use. They should make notes in the appropriate boxes on photocopiable page 151, completing a separate copy of the page for each settlement (there are two settlements featured per programme).

After each programme, discuss as a class what has been learned about the settlements.

Part 2: writing an article about change in settlements (about 1 hour)

When all the programmes have been watched, children work in mixed-ability groups of four to six (allocating tasks between themselves) to produce a draft article for 'The Planner's Gazette', which describes and explains changes within the settlements investigated. Each group should focus on a pair of settlements, as featured in one of the programmes. They use the notes they have made on copies of photocopiable page 151 to help them construct their reports, plus other secondary sources of information. They should decide between themselves which members of the group should carry out which tasks, and list the sources of additional information they will use to research their article. They should present their work using a word-processing package.

Plenary
As a class, summarise through discussion what has been learned about how and why settlements change over time.

Differentiation
Less able children could be provided with a writing frame for their report for 'The Planner's Gazette', though they will be working in mixed-ability groups, and so should be supported by other children.

Assessing learning outcomes
Ephemeral evidence
● Observation of, and listening to, the children's discussion as they carry out the report-writing activity.
● Questions asked by the children and answers given to questions framed by the teacher.
● Geographical vocabulary used by the children when undertaking the activity.
● Teamwork and co-operation – how well do the children work together in groups?
Retainable evidence
● Children's responses to the relevance and accuracy of evidence recorded by the children about change in settlements on photocopiable page 151.
● Children's reports for 'The Planner's Gazette'.

ICT opportunities
Children could access additional information using the Internet and CD-ROMs to assist them with their article for 'The Planner's Gazette'.

Follow-up activity
Children could choose one of the settlements studied and think about how its character and function might continue to change in the future.

CHAPTER 4
SETTLEMENTS

Using television
to support the
study of
settlements

How and why has our settlement changed?

(1 hour 30 mins)

What you need and preparation

Before this lesson, audit and develop your knowledge about your own settlement. Use the following points as a guide (see 'Background information' for the units on 'Contrasting localities' and 'Investigating settlements' on pages 19 and 72 for definitions of the terms):

● Settlement hierarchy – where is your settlement in the settlement hierarchy?

● Site and situation – what are the features of the site of your settlement (that is, the physical profile of the land your settlement is on)? Why did people originally settle here? Are there any clues about who the original settlers were? Where is your settlement located within the region/country/Europe?

● Size – how big is your settlement in terms of population and area? Is population increasing or decreasing?

● Shape – is your settlement linear, dispersed or nucleated? Does the shape of the settlement relate to its function?

● Function – what are the main economic activities in your settlement in the past and in the present?

● Land-use – what are the main land-uses in your settlement?

Arrange for a planner from your local Planning Office to visit the school to talk to the children about the role of the planner in deciding how settlements are developed, and the constraints within which they work. The planner should also help answer children's questions about their own settlement. Write to your local Planning Office beforehand to request a visit, and to brief the planner on what to expect! Depending on when the visit can be arranged, the introduction to this lesson may have to be carried out on a separate occasion to the rest of the lesson.

You will need: maps, photographs and other sources of information about your own settlement and the way it has changed over the last 100 years, to including historical maps, copies of which may be obtained from a local Records Office, and contemporary Ordnance Survey maps (1:50 000).

Learning objectives
● Ask geographical questions.
● Collect and record evidence.
● Analyse evidence and draw conclusions.
● Communicate in ways appropriate to the task and audience.
● Use appropriate geographical vocabulary.
● Use secondary sources of information.
● Use ICT to help in geographical investigations.
● Use decision-making skills.
● Learn about UK localities.
● Investigate an environmental issue.
● Recognise how and why people may seek to manage environments sustainably.
● Identify and explain different views that people, including themselves, hold about topical geographical issues.

Lesson organisation
Initial brainstorming session in which children work in small, mixed-ability groups to list the changes in their own settlement. Teacher-led discussion with the whole class, during which the class compiles a list of questions about how and why their settlement has changed to ask a visiting town planner. Whole-class 'question and answer' session with visiting planner, possibly on a separate occasion. Plenary session at the end.

What to do

Introduction
(10 mins) Introduce the lesson by discussing with the children ways in which their own settlement may have changed over time. If their families come from the settlement, do their parents or grandparents say things have changed in the local area? What do the children know about the way the settlement was a hundred years ago?

In mixed-ability groups of four to six, the children use historical and contemporary maps, plus other sources of local information (photographs, maps of town centre, historical booklets), to brainstorm obvious changes to their own settlement. They could use the following headings to help organise their ideas: land-use, physical features, human features, size, shape, economic activities.

Discuss as a class the role of planners in deciding how settlements change. Compile a list of questions that the children would like to ask a planner (based on the examples of change that they identified in the brainstorming session, as well as their own knowledge of the settlement). For example:

Vocabulary
settlement
hamlet
village
town
city
conurbation
linear
nucleated
dispersed
land-use
function
commercial
industrial
manufacturing
economic activity
site
situation

Using television to support the study of settlements

● Why did the council build a car park there?
● Why is access to the city centre (by road) restricted?

Children should record their main concerns about past and future changes in their settlement, and devise questions for the planner to try to answer their concerns.

Explain to the children the focus of the rest of the lesson:

● to find out the nature of and reasons for change in their own settlement
● to evaluate and respond to changes.

① Development
1 hour
When the planner visits, he or she should talk to the children about the role of the planner in deciding how settlements are built and developed, and what constraints the planner works within. Following the talk, the children should take turns to ask the questions compiled by the class during the introduction session. The questions could be divided up among the children beforehand, so that they all understand what they are going to ask. They could also ask general questions about what the planner does day-to-day. The children should make notes of the planner's responses to their questions, and could make a display afterwards showing particularly important quotes.

After the discussion, children should write a letter to the local Planning Office outlining how decisions already made have affected their lives, and the impact that future developments may have.

Plenary
20 mins
As a class, summarise the children's main areas of interest or concern about changes in the settlement. Discuss the planner's responses to questions on these points.

Differentiation
This lesson is accessible to children of all abilities. The group work is undertaken in mixed-ability groups. Ensure the questions are worded appropriately for the children asking them, so that they understand clearly what they are asking the planner.

Assessing learning outcomes
Ephemeral evidence
● Observation of, and listening to, the children's questions and responses to answers during the planner's visit.
● Geographical vocabulary used by the children when devising and asking questions.
● Teamwork and co-operation – how well do the children work together in groups during the introductory brainstorming activity?

Retainable evidence
● Children's list of questions for the planner.
● Children's letters to the local planning department about settlement changes.

Environmental Change

Introduction

The Programme of Study for children at Key Stage 2, in the National Curriculum (2000), includes the aspect of knowledge and understanding of environmental change and sustainable development. It is stated that children should be taught to 'recognise how people can improve the environment or damage it and how decisions about places and environments affect the future quality of people's lives' (5a), and to 'recognise how and why people may seek to manage environments sustainably, and to identify opportunities for their own involvement' (5b). In its section on Breadth of Study, the Programme of Study makes specific reference to the teaching of knowledge, skills and understanding through the study of two localities and three themes. One of the themes includes helping children to learn about 'attempts to manage the environment sustainably' (6e).

The following two units of work in this chapter provide ideal opportunities not only for developing knowledge and understanding of environmental change and sustainable development and for investigating ways to 'manage the environment sustainably' (6e), but also for incorporating aspects of a study of the children's immediate locality, 'a locality in the United Kingdom' (6a) and 'a locality in a country that is less economically developed' (6b).

Three aspects of geography can also be taught through the theme of environmental change:

● **Geographical enquiry and skills** – for example, children use secondary sources to identify evidence of change in environments.

● **Knowledge and understanding of places** – for example, children develop a framework of locational knowledge through study of different places and environments.

● **Knowledge and understanding of patterns and processes** – for example, children develop ideas about the effects of physical and human processes on environments.

The first unit in this chapter, 'Sustainability 'through the window'', uses the view from the classroom window to focus the children's work on their immediate environment. The aims of Agenda 21 and the key principles of sustainable development are introduced to the children and developed. The children may even be familiar with the 'Local Agenda 21' initiative, as this has been implemented at local authority level, trying to involve local communities across the country.

The second unit, 'What happens to all that waste?', raises issues about the amounts of waste generated by modern life, how we dispose of this waste and the consequences. The unit tries to help children recognise that their actions at a local level can make a difference to global environmental problems and contribute towards sustainable development. The ways in which the disposal of rubbish is managed, and the ways in which the amount of waste produced by each one of us can be reduced, are investigated. The '4 Rs' of rubbish minimisation are introduced and issues about siting landfill sites are investigated. This unit provides an ideal opportunity to investigate 'an environmental issue, caused by change in an environment...' (6e) and 'an issue arising from changes in land-use' (6d). The unit provides opportunities for children to explore their responsibilities as members of the community (citizenship) and to investigate sustainable developments with regard to waste management, use of the Earth's limited resources, and pollution.

This chapter aims to provide opportunities to acquire the knowledge, understanding and skills necessary to become actively and effectively involved in environmental issues, particularly those aiming to create and manage sustainable environments. It includes activities that aim to help children learn how to make sense of some environmental issues through direct experience, and by adopting a sensitive approach to take into account conflicting interests and different viewpoints.

The units in this chapter build on units in QCA's *A Scheme of Work for Key Stages 1 and 2*, expanding on QCA's Unit 20, 'Local traffic – an environmental issue', Unit 21, 'How can we improve the area we can see from our window?', and Unit 8, 'Improving the environment'. There are links between this chapter and Chapter 2, where issues of sustainability are raised in comparing different forms of transport in India with the UK. There is also a lesson where children consider the creativity and resourcefulness with which people re-use waste in less economically developed countries.

Sustainability 'through the window'

Background information

Sustainable development is centrally concerned with reducing pressure on the environment caused by human activities, protecting all forms of wildlife, promoting the wiser use of resources and reducing pollution. Agenda 21 represents a global plan of action for the 21st century (established at the Rio Summit, 1992) and embraces the key principles of sustainable development. The 'Local Agenda 21' initiative has been implemented at local authority level, and the following eight key themes have been identified:

- **transport** – aiming to encourage the use of more sustainable modes of transport
- **energy** – aiming to decrease the use of household and commercial energy
- **land-use** – aiming to decelerate the process of urbanisation and outward growth
- **water** – aiming to avoid waste and to improve the quality of natural water systems
- **air** – aiming to reduce the level of air pollution
- **waste** – aiming to reduce waste, to re-use materials and to recycle
- **wildlife** – aiming to maintain and promote diversity
- **landscape** – aiming to maintain and promote diversity of plants and trees in particular.

Targets relating to each of these areas have been set by local authorities and indicators have been identified so as to monitor improvements.

In this unit children consider, in particular, issues relating to sustainable transport. Focusing on the relatively small area of the locality visible from the classroom window, children are able to undertake in-depth research and analysis of transport issues in which they may be directly involved. The series of four lessons explores the issue of carbon dioxide emissions (from motorised vehicles) and ways in which more sustainable modes of transport (including public transport, walking and cycling) can be encouraged.

UNIT: Sustainability 'through the window'

Enquiry questions	Teaching objectives	Teaching activities	Learning outcomes	Cross curricular links
What is sustainable development? What is Agenda 21? What are the key target areas?	• Use appropriate geographical vocabulary. • Investigate an environmental issue. • Recognise how and why people may seek to manage environments sustainably.	Discuss with the children the notion of Agenda 21 and list the eight key themes, explaining why such issues should concern them. Children complete photocopiable page 152 with a view to increasing their awareness of such issues. (This can be used as a form of baseline assessment.)	Children: • can identify key target areas of Agenda 21.	
What is sustainable transport? What is the view from the window like? How does it change over time, and how does this make us feel? What is the process causing these changes? What are sustainable modes of transport?	• Ask geographical questions. • Collect and record evidence. • Use appropriate geographical vocabulary. • Investigate an environmental issue, caused by change in an environment, and attempts to manage the environment sustainably. • Recognise some human processes and explain how these can cause changes in environments. • Recognise how people can improve the environment or damage it. • Recognise how people and places fit within a wider geographical context and are interdependent.	Children recap on what they think 'sustainability' means. Show a series of three images of the same area over time, showing more and more evidence of transport – more traffic, and more variety of vehicles. Children write down one adjective and one statement that describes how they feel about the scene in each image, on photocopiable page 153. Identify patterns in the children's responses and discuss which features and processes have affected them. Link this to the transport evident, and discuss more and less sustainable modes of transport. Children design a questionnaire using photocopiable page 153, and use it to survey children about how they travel to school.	• can use adjectives to describe the environment. understand what is meant by sustainable modes of transport. • can produce a questionnaire to find out how people travel to school each day and why they use the modes of transport that they do.	Literacy: use of adjectives
How do different children travel to school? Are people more likely to use less sustainable modes of transport than more sustainable modes? If so, why? How can we change people's attitudes and behaviours?	• Ask geographical questions. • Analyse evidence and draw conclusions. • Use ICT to help in geographical investigations. • Communicate in ways appropriate to the task and audience. • Use appropriate geographical vocabulary. • Use maps and plans. • Use decision-making skills. • Investigate an environmental issue, caused by change in an environment, and attempts to manage the environment sustainably. • Recognise some human processes and explain how these can cause changes in environments. • Recognise how people can improve the environment or damage it. • Recognise how people and places fit within a wider geographical context and are interdependent.	Using ICT, children analyse and present the data they obtained using their questionnaires from the previous lesson ('What is sustainable transport?'). They illustrate recommendations to promote the use of more sustainable transport (eg cycle lanes on road to school) on a large scale base map of the school and local area. Children may choose to forward their findings to the local planning office using a writing frame.	• can present and analyse data using ICT and base maps. • understand the implications of the data and make recommendations encouraging the use of more sustainable modes of transport.	ICT: word-processing and spreadsheets to present and analyse questionnaire data Literacy: use of a writing frame
What might a more sustainable future look like? What is the view like from our window? How might it change?	• Ask geographical questions. • Use appropriate geographical vocabulary. • Use appropriate fieldwork techniques. • Learn about a UK locality. • Investigate an environmental issue, caused by change in an environment, and attempts to manage the environment sustainably. • Recognise some human processes and explain how these can cause changes in environments.	Using photocopiable page 155, children field sketch the view from their classroom window, adding notes to identify human and physical features, as well as any evidence of sustainable development (eg recycling bins, bus stops). They then add notes and illustrations to show how they think developments could be made towards a more sustainable way of life in the local area.	• can produce a field sketch. • develop an understanding of sustainable transport.	

Resources

Window by Jeannie Baker (published by Red Fox, ISBN 0 09 91821 4), or a series of photographs based on the view from a window at different points through time, to show changes in traffic; *Transport: towards a more sustainable lifestyle* published by the Tidy Britain Group (1998) and free to all schools; copies of the children's questionnaires, once completed; children of different ages to survey on transport using the children's own questionnaires; raw data from transport questionnaire; access to Internet; access to computers with word-processing, spreadsheets and data-handling software; large-scale base maps of school and local area; writing frame to help children construct proposals for the local planning office; classroom (or other) window with a view including a range of features (such as roads and traffic, crossings, vegetation, buildings, hills); pencils; photocopiable pages 152–155.

CHAPTER 5
ENVIRONMENTAL
CHANGE

**Sustainability
'through the
window'**

(30 mins) What is sustainable development?

**Learning
objectives**
● Use appropriate
geographical
vocabulary.
● Investigate an
environmental
issue.
● Recognise how
and why people
may seek to
manage
environments
sustainably.

**Lesson
organisation**
Initial teacher-led
discussion with the
whole class on
sustainable
development,
followed by a short
activity in which
children work
individually to
complete
photocopiable page
152, considering
how their actions
can affect the
environment.
Whole-class
plenary session at
the end.

Vocabulary
sustainability
environment
resources
Agenda 21
transport
energy
land-use
water
air
waste
wildlife
landscape

What you need and preparation
You will need: a copy of photocopiable page 152 for each child.

What to do

(10 mins) Introduction
Introduce the lesson to the whole class by asking the children what they think 'sustainability'
means (talk about the verb 'to sustain'). A possible definition may include the notion of developing
practices that help to sustain the environment and which consider the needs of future generations.
   Explain to the children the focus of the lesson:
● to introduce the concept of sustainability within the context of a global plan of action
(Agenda 21)
● to introduce the key themes of Agenda 21
● to consider actions that may be taken at a personal level.

(10 mins) Development
Discuss the fact that issues relating to sustainable development are not easily resolved and
require global, long-term initiatives to bring about significant change. Discuss how global action
has to start locally and at the level of individual action. Introduce Agenda 21 (see 'Background
information' on page 92) and discuss each of the eight themes with the children.
   Ask the children to complete photocopiable page 152, working individually. In doing so, they
consider how their personal actions affect the environment, and how modifying their actions might
contribute to the targets set for each theme by the local authority.

(10 mins) Plenary
Discuss children's responses to photocopiable page 152 and consider the impacts of
individual and collective actions; for example, the impact of sorting and recycling rubbish in the
home and in school.

Differentiation
This is an open-ended activity, which may be used as a form of baseline assessment.

CHAPTER 5
ENVIRONMENTAL
CHANGE

Sustainability
'through the
window'

Assessing learning outcomes

Ephemeral evidence

● Observation of, and listening to, the children's discussion as they complete the activity.

● Questions asked by the children and answers given to questions framed by the teacher.

● Geographical vocabulary used by the children when undertaking the activity.

● Children's ideas about sustainability.

Retainable evidence

● Children's completed photocopiable page 152.

ICT opportunities
Children could use the Internet to find out more about Agenda 21 and sustainable development.

Follow-up activity
Children could write to their Local Authority to find out more about their specific targets for the 'Local Agenda 21' initiative.

1 hour — What is sustainable transport?

What you need and preparation

You will need: a copy of the book entitled *Window* by Jeannie Baker (Red Fox, ISBN 0 09 91821 4), or a series of images (pictures or photographs) based on the view from a particular window at different points through time, to show changes in traffic volume and variations in the modes of transport visible (select three images that show a clear increase in the amount of traffic over time); a copy of *Transport: Towards a More Sustainable Lifestyle* from the Tidy Britain Group (1998) and free to all schools; a copy of photocopiable pages 152 and 153 for each child; copies of the children's questionnaires once completed; samples of children of different ages from throughout the school, to survey on transport using the children's own questionnaires.

What to do

10 mins — Introduction

Introduce the lesson to the whole class by asking the children to recap on what they understand by the term 'sustainability'.

Explain to the children the focus of the lesson:

● to introduce the concept of environment (including rural and urban contrasts)

● to develop the concept of sustainability, focusing on sustainable modes of transport

● to collect data to help to explain issues surrounding transport and to develop possible ways forward towards sustainable transport.

40 mins — Development

Explain to the children that they will be shown a series of three images taken from a window (if you are using images from the book *Window* by Jeannie Baker, show the children the book). They should write down three adjectives ('describing words') that come to mind when they view each image. For example, they might suggest 'peaceful', 'urban', 'busy' or 'vandalised'. Ask the children to write down one statement on photocopiable page 152 about each image which describes how they feel about it.

Identify patterns in the children's responses and discuss which features and processes cause the children to give positive or negative responses. Link this to the idea that the images progressively show more evidence of motor traffic.

Discuss the notion of more and less sustainable forms of transport. More sustainable modes of transport include walking, cycling and use of public transport, because they involve a reduction in

Learning objectives
● Ask geographical questions.
● Collect and record evidence.
● Use appropriate geographical vocabulary.
● Investigate an environmental issue, caused by change in an environment, and attempts to manage the environment sustainably.
● Recognise some human processes and explain how these can cause changes in environments.
● Recognise how people can improve the environment or damage it.
● Recognise how people and places fit within a wider geographical context and are interdependent.

Lesson organisation
Initial teacher-led discussion with whole class about sustainability, particularly with respect to transport, followed by work in pairs of similar ability on photocopiable page 153. Whole-class plenary session at the end on analysing and presenting data.

Vocabulary
sustainability
environment
resources
Agenda 21
transport
energy
land-use
water
air
waste
wildlife
landscape
train
bus
tram
cycle lanes
routes

the overall use of fossil fuel, and consequently a reduction in carbon dioxide emissions, which are linked to the issue of global warming.

It is important to explain that there are no immediate solutions to environmental problems. Modern lifestyles do not encourage sustainable practices. For example, there is often a lack of public transport, particularly in more rural areas, and urban areas have been planned and developed over recent decades to accommodate car owners and car use. It is equally as important to emphasise that attitudes and behaviours need to change in the long term if environmental problems are not to worsen.

Tell the children that they are going to design a questionnaire to collect evidence so that they can find out why more children don't travel to school on foot, by bicycle or by public transport (sustainable modes of transport). It is important to emphasise that the aim of the exercise is not to apportion blame, but to move towards real recommendations for ways to encourage more people to use sustainable transport relating to the school and its catchment area.

Let the children work in pairs to design their questionnaires, using photocopiable page 153, and then use them to interview a selected sample of children across different age groups about how they travel to school. (They could interview children during break times, or special arrangements could be made for small groups to go into other lessons for a short time to interview the children there.)

(10 mins) Plenary

Evaluate different methods of data collection, and discuss possible strategies for presenting and handling data on transport. (Children will analyse and present the data they obtain using their questionnaires in the next lesson.)

Differentiation

Children should work in pairs of similar ability.

Less able children could be provided with examples of possible questions for inclusion in their questionnaire (see *Transport: Towards a More Sustainable Lifestyle*, from the Tidy Britain Group (1998) and free to all schools). Use human resources (classroom assistants/voluntary helpers), if available, to work with less able children.

Assessing learning outcomes

Ephemeral evidence

- Observation of, and listening to, the children's discussion as they work on their questionnaires.
- Questions asked by the children and answers given to questions framed by the teacher.
- Geographical vocabulary used by the children when undertaking the activity.
- Children's ideas about sustainable modes of transport.
- Teamwork and co-operation – how well do the children work together in pairs?

Retainable evidence

- Children's adjectives and statements about the pictures on photocopiable page 152.
- Children's questionnaires, and the raw data they collect.

ICT opportunities
- Children could present their questionnaires using a word-processing package, and print off as many copies as they need.
- Children could use the Internet to find out about public transport in other countries, both within Europe and beyond.

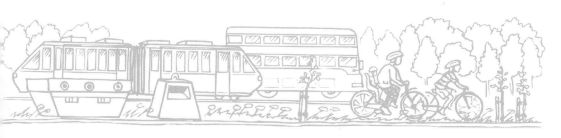

CHAPTER 5
ENVIRONMENTAL
CHANGE

Sustainability
'through the
window'

1 hour 10 mins How do different children travel to school?

What you need and preparation
You will need: access to computers with word-processing, spreadsheet and data-handling software; large-scale base maps of the school and local area; raw data from questionnaire survey carried out from the previous lesson ('What is sustainable transport?', on page 95); writing frame to help children construct proposals for the local planning office.

What to do

10 mins Introduction
Introduce the lesson by reminding children that they have collected data in order to establish how children travel to school, and why more children don't travel on foot, by bicycle or by public transport (sustainable modes of transport). Re-emphasise that the aim of the exercise is not to apportion blame, but to move towards real recommendations for ways to encourage more people to use sustainable transport, relating to the school and its catchment area.

Ask the children about the raw data they obtained using the questionnaires produced in the previous lesson ('What is sustainable transport?', on page 95), and how they might choose to analyse and present the data using ICT. Remind the children of the software available on the school computers and discuss the appropriateness of each different package.

Explain to the children the focus of the lesson:
● to decide how best to analyse and present the data collected on modes of transport taken to school, using the ICT facilities available
● to analyse the data and to make recommendations with a view to promoting sustainable modes of transport.

50 mins Development
Ask the children to present and analyse the data collected on modes of transport taken to school, using ICT. The children should be involved in decision-making about which software to use for presenting and analysing. For example, they could use:
● a table to summarise the sample structure (age / sex / name)
● a database to show age / sex / mode of transport used (sustainable / not sustainable) / reasons for use / if by car, why not walk? / if by car, why not cycle? / if by car, why not use public transport?
● a pie chart to show all the modes of transport used by the whole sample
● a graph to show the numbers of children using more sustainable or less sustainable modes of transport overall
● a table summarising reasons for not walking / cycling / using public transport for children who travel to school by car.
In analysing their data, children should be encouraged to consider:
● whether age, gender, or other factors relate to the mode of transport used
● what proportion of the sample use less sustainable modes of transport
● if the proportion is large, reasons why so few children walk, cycle or use public transport.
Children should then make recommendations based on their data analysis for ways in which to encourage people to use more sustainable modes of transport. For example, they might suggest having cycle lanes on the main roads to the school. They should illustrate their suggestions on a

Learning objectives
● Ask geographical questions.
● Analyse evidence and draw conclusions.
● Use ICT to help in geographical investigations.
● Communicate in ways appropriate to the task and audience.
● Use appropriate geographical vocabulary.
● Use maps and plans.
● Use decision-making skills.
● Investigate an environmental issue, caused by change in an environment, and attempts to manage the environment sustainably.
● Recognise some human processes and explain how these can cause changes in environments.
● Recognise how people can improve the environment or damage it.
● Recognise how people and places fit within a wider geographical context and are interdependent.

Lesson organisation
Initial teacher-led discussion with whole class, followed by paired activity, either taking turns on a single classroom computer, or working simultaneously in a computer suite. (If children are to take turns using ICT, this lesson must be scheduled alongside other curriculum activities for the rest of the class.) Whole-class plenary session when all pairs have completed the task.

Vocabulary
sustainability
environment
resources
Agenda 21
transport
energy
land-use
water
air
waste
wildlife
landscape

Sustainability 'through the window'

ICT opportunities
Children use word-processing and spreadsheets to analyse and present their data on modes of transport.

Follow-up activity
Children could design and make posters to be displayed around the school to promote more sustainable modes of transport.

large-scale base map of the school and local area, and could communicate their findings and ideas to the local planning office using a writing frame.

Plenary
10 mins
Discuss as a class all the recommendations and proposals that have been illustrated on the base map. Get the children to think about how easy it would be to install each suggestion, and how effective they might prove to be in the short and long term. Can they think of any reasons why these ideas have not been put in place already by the local planning office?

Differentiation
Children should work in pairs of similar ability.

Less able children could be provided with support on deciding how to analyse and present their data, and encouraged to work with a smaller data set (for example, the results of perhaps just five or six questionnaires). Use human resources (classroom assistants/voluntary helpers), if available, to work with less able children.

Assessing learning outcomes
Ephemeral evidence
● Observation of, and listening to, children's discussion as they analyse and present their data.
● Questions asked by the children and answers given to questions framed by the teacher.
● Geographical vocabulary used by the children when undertaking the activity.
● Children's ideas about sustainability and how to promote it.
● Teamwork and co-operation – how well do the children work together in pairs?

Retainable evidence
● Children's presentation and analysis of data, in the form of computer-generated work.
● The class base map, showing proposals to promote sustainability.
● Letters written to local planning office, with proposals.

What might a more sustainable future look like?
1 hour

Learning objectives
● Ask geographical questions.
● Use appropriate geographical vocabulary.
● Use appropriate fieldwork techniques.
● Learn about a UK locality.
● Investigate an environmental issue, caused by change in an environment, and attempts to manage the environment sustainably.
● Recognise some human processes and explain how these can cause changes in environments.
● Recognise how people can improve the environment or damage it.
● Recognise how people and places fit within a wider geographical context and are interdependent.

Lesson organisation
Initial teacher-led discussion with whole class, followed by individual field-sketch activity (within small groups). Whole-class plenary session when all pupils have completed the task.

What you need and preparation
You will need: classroom (or other) window with a view that can be seen clearly by the children and which includes a range of features (such as roads and traffic, crossings, vegetation, buildings, hills); pencils; a copy of *Window* by Jeannie Baker (Red Fox, ISBN 0 09 91821 4), or a series of images (pictures or photographs) based on the view from a particular window at different points through time, to show changes in traffic volume and variations in the modes of transport visible; a copy of photocopiable page 155 for each child.

What to do
Introduction
10 mins
Explain to the children the focus of the lesson:
● to relate the children's previous learning about sustainability and traffic, and their survey findings, to the school grounds and the local area
● to complete a field sketch of the view from a window
● to consider how the view from the window might be developed to reflect more sustainable lifestyles.

Sustainability 'through the window'

Discuss the aims of field sketching: to record relevant information quickly and accurately using illustrations, notes and clear labels.

(40 mins) Development

Use the book *Window* by Jeannie Baker, or your series of photographs showing increasing intensity of traffic over time, to recap on environmental issues and the concept of sustainability. In small groups, ask the children to look through the classroom window (or another window elsewhere in the school, if more appropriate) and to list what they can see in terms of physical and human features, using photocopiable page 155. Ask them also to note down any evidence of sustainable development; for example, recycling bins or units, cycle lanes, bus stops and so on.

Ask the children to complete a field sketch of the view, also on photocopiable page 155. Then they should add labels and additional illustrations to show how they think things could be changed in order to help develop sustainability.

(10 mins) Plenary

As a class, discuss what the children can see already through the window in terms of sustainability, and the views they would like to see in the future.

Differentiation

This lesson is accessible to children of all abilities. Children should work independently, within mixed-ability groups.

Assessing learning outcomes

Ephemeral evidence

- Observation of, and listening to, the children's discussion as they analyse the view and make a field sketch of it.
- Questions asked by the children and answers given to questions framed by the teacher.
- Geographical vocabulary used by the children when undertaking the activity.
- Children's ideas about sustainability and how to promote it.

Retainable evidence

- Children's annotated field sketches, which illustrate examples of sustainable development.

Vocabulary
sustainability
environment
resources
Agenda 21
transport
energy
land-use
water
air
waste
wildlife
landscape
human and
physical features
residential
industrial
(industry)

ICT opportunities
If suitable software is available, children could scan in a photograph of the view from the window, and manipulate it to see what it might look like in a more sustainable future. For example, they could scan in an image of a tram, and superimpose it onto a main road. They could add sorting and recycling bins, pedestrians and cyclists, and perhaps even remove cars and lorries.

Follow-up activity
Children could produce a whole-class display of the view through the window, annotated with the children's main proposals for development, agreed through whole-class discussion.

CHAPTER 5
ENVIRONMENTAL
CHANGE

What happens to all that waste?

Background information

Waste is created everywhere – at home, at school, in factories and in offices. We all create waste and throw all sorts of things into our dustbins. In fact each one of us throws away about ten times our own weight in household rubbish annually. More than a third of the rubbish generated by UK households is packaging, and the average family gets through nearly 10 kilograms of it every week. Each day, the United Kingdom produces enough rubbish to fill Trafalgar Square to the top of Nelson's Column and each year the average UK family throws out waste paper that it took six trees to make. Altogether in the UK we throw away seven million drinks cans every year.

Some items of waste can be re-used or recycled but others cannot; for example, polystyrene. Recycling means converting waste (such as newspapers, aluminium cans and so on) into materials that can be used again. It involves processes that require energy. Re-use means to use again, as with second-hand clothes or books (distributed through charity shops, jumble sales and so on). The rules for waste minimisation – the '4 Rs' – are shown below:

● Avoid making unnecessary waste wherever possible, by not taking supermarket carrier bags, and not buying goods with unnecessary packaging (**Refuse**). Re-using and recycling are good ideas, but it is much better not to make waste in the first place!

● Re-use as much waste as possible (**Re-use**). Re-using is better than recycling. When something is recycled it usually needs quite a lot of energy to turn it into something new.

● Where waste cannot be re-used, recycle as much as possible (**Recycle**). Recycling things saves the world's resources. It also takes less energy to recycle things than to make them from raw materials.

● If waste cannot be re-used or recycled, make it take up less space, for example by using it for fuel (**Reduce**). If waste is used for fuel, it saves using more of the dwindling reserves of fossil fuels (coal, oil, gas). It also reduces the amount of waste that has to be disposed of.

Any waste that cannot be used usefully in any way should be disposed of in the way that is least damaging to the environment.

The most common disposal method for household rubbish is in landfill sites. Around 90% of household waste goes to landfill, with the remaining 10% being incinerated. Both methods of waste disposal impact on the environment. Landfill sites (often in old quarries, railway cuttings, shallow valleys and so on) can cause problems if not well managed – smells, wind-blown refuse, flies, rats, acidic run-off, methane gas and so on. Incineration of waste emits toxic fumes and smoke.

Using landfill sites to dispose of waste has been the easy and cheap option, but as more sites are filled up, waste has to be transported further, increasing both the economic and environmental cost of the practice.

Currently, a lot of work is being done by local authorities to reduce the amount of waste being produced and to increase waste treatment and recycling. Reducing domestic waste has the effect of extending the life of landfill sites – new sites are not needed so quickly. However, for the foreseeable future, landfill will still be necessary for residual waste.

The stages in the life of a landfill 'cell' are set out below. (A site often consists of several 'cells', at different stages of development – some in preparation, some in operation, and some undergoing restoration.)

● **Preparation** – removal and storage of top- and sub-soil from an area, and excavation of the hollow. The pit is then lined with clay and a protective lining to prevent poisonous substances (leachate) from the decomposing waste being washed onto the land and waterways around the site.

● **Operation** – the site is progressively filled with waste material, which is compacted and quickly covered.

● **Restoration** – waste is sealed, sub- and top-soil are replaced and the area is landscaped (using sympathetic contouring, new trees and shrubs, and so on) to create woodland, farmland, recreational facilities such as golf courses and so on.

The issue of proposed sites for new landfill always causes grave concerns and emotional outcries amongst the residents of the area concerned. Although landfill is widespread, and is the most popular waste disposal method because it is the cheapest, it has its problems:

● people do not want landfill sites near where they live

● as waste decays it gives off landfill gas (methane), which can be dangerous (even explosive)

● great care has to be taken to make sure poisons (leachate) do not leak from the site and contaminate surrounding water and land

● landfill sites are usually quite a long way from towns and cities, which means many heavy lorries carrying waste travel quite long distances.

This unit includes an issue-based role-play activity. This type of activity – which involves children developing a role and empathising with that role – helps the children to see other people's points of view. It also encourages the children to begin to think about what sort of action they could become involved in to ensure that their opinions are heard and considered along with the viewpoints of others. This helps the children to develop their roles as active, responsible citizens.

All over the world, especially in less economically developed countries, many people make their living from rubbish. Some people search through rubbish dumps, looking through the waste that others throw away for anything that they can sell to earn a living or anything they can use to make goods either for themselves or to sell. It may seem like a good thing that these people recycle all the useful rubbish so that less goes to waste, but their lives are unpleasant and dangerous. There are hazardous substances in the waste, which can make people ill and even kill them. There are also diseases carried by rats and flies that live on the dumps.

This unit of work will help children to think about how much waste each one of us produces and to investigate ways of reducing this mountain of waste by simple actions we can all adopt. The issues of waste disposal and its impact on the environment are investigated. The wasting of raw materials, resources and energy to produce some of the items we throw away is also examined.

Children are very interested in and concerned about the state of the planet on which they live. This unit looks at the management of waste, and aims to help children become more aware of the consequences of the actions they take towards waste generation and disposal today, in their future and beyond. Children need to realise that what each one of them does today has a direct impact on the future. 'Think Globally, Act Locally' is a message for everyone to take on board. We must not just make children aware of concerns and issues, but help them to develop the confidence and desire to become active citizens.

UNIT: What happens to all that waste?

Enquiry questions	Teaching objectives	Teaching activities	Learning outcomes	Cross-curricular links
What do we throw away? What kinds of things do people throw away? What are these things made of? How could we re-use some of these things?	● Recognise how people can improve the environment or damage it. ● Collect and record evidence. ● Analyse evidence and draw conclusions. ● Use ICT. ● Recognise how and why people may seek to manage environments sustainably, and to identify opportunities for their own involvement. ● Investigate attempts to manage the environment sustainably. ● Use appropriate fieldwork techniques.	Children demonstrate what they know about waste management using concept mapping. Children brainstorm and categorise items of rubbish. They then design a data collection sheet and carry out a simple survey to investigate the amount of rubbish thrown away in school over one lunchtime. They record, present and analyse the data using ICT. Using photocopiable page 156 and data collected in the survey, children consider actions that individuals could take to reduce the amount of rubbish created.	Children: ● can construct a simple data-collection sheet to find out what is thrown away. ● can undertake a simple survey to collect data, and analyse and use that data. ● are able to use secondary data and their own data to consider what each one of us could do to reduce the amount of rubbish.	ICT: data collection sheet, spreadsheet Numeracy: analysis of materials, sorting into categories
How can we be less wasteful? How can we reduce how much we throw away? How does refusing, re-using, recycling and reducing help the environment?	● Recognise how people can improve the environment or damage it. ● Recognise how and why people seek to create and manage sustainable environments and to identify opportunities for their own involvement. Investigate attempts to manage the environment sustainably.	Introduce the '4 Rs' of rubbish minimisation - refuse, re-use, recycle and reduce, and discuss. In groups, children sort cleaned waste into categories according to how it can be re-used, recycled etc (discussed by the children). They discuss how doing these things will help the environment. Children play the 'Waste not, want not' game (photocopiable page 157). They discuss penalties and bonuses for undertaking certain actions when landing on some squares.	● know the '4 Rs' of rubbish minimisation - refuse, re-use, recycle and reduce. can sort rubbish into different categories according to how it can be dealt with as an item of waste. ● develop an understanding of how refusing, re-using, recycling and reducing helps the environment.	Science: properties of materials, sorting into categories
What happens at a landfill site? Where is the landfill site? Why is this landfill located here? How can I ensure I am safe when I visit the site? Does the site affect the community?	● Recognise how people can improve the environment or damage it. ● Recognise how and why people seek to create and manage sustainable environments and to identify opportunities for their own involvement. ● Investigate attempts to manage the environment sustainably. ● Use appropriate fieldwork techniques.	Discuss what a landfill site is. In groups, children locate the landfill site to be visited on maps and aerial photographs. They plan a route to the site, considering what criteria for 'best route' to use? The class discusses health and safety issues, and designs a set of safety rules for the visit. During the visit, children find out how the cells are made and filled in, any affects the site has on the local community, how the land is returned to fields, forests and walks. Back in school, children write reports of the site visit using photocopiable 158. Their written work could be displayed in a large dustbin shaped book.	● are able to use maps to plan a 'best route', explaining the criteria used. ● are aware of the dangers of a landfill site and can develop and follow a safety code of conduct. ● can explain how a landfill site operates. ● appreciate how an area is changing and how landfill will affect what the land is used for in the future.	Literacy: recount genre
What do other people do with their rubbish? What happens to rubbish in less economically developed countries? What are the dangers and benefits of people making a living from rubbish?	● Recognise how people can improve the environment or damage it. ● Recognise some human processes and explain how these can cause changes in places and environments. ● Recognise how and why people seek to create and manage sustainable environments and to identify opportunities for their own involvement. ● Investigate attempts to manage the environment sustainably.	Recap on re-using and recycling waste in the UK. Discuss how some people, particularly in less economically developed countries, make their living by sorting through waste looking for items to recycling or re-use. Discuss the dangers and benefits of this lifestyle. Children handle and discuss artefacts made from recycled materials. For each article, they complete photocopiable page 159, and locate the country of origin on a world map or globe. In small groups or pairs, children design and make clothes out of waste products. Later, they could present the 'Waste Clothes Show', which could be photographed.	● understand the use made of rubbish in economically less developed countries and the dangers of this type of lifestyle. ● appreciate the creativity and ingenuity involved in some of the items made from re-used rubbish. ● use their own creative talents to design and make clothes from waste.	Art, Design and Technology: clothes made out of waste
Where shall we build a new landfill site? How would you feel if a landfill site was developed in your area? Who would you contact about this? Where would you get information? How would you express your veiws?	● Recognise how people can improve the environment or damage it, and how decisions about places and environments affect the future quality of people's lives. ● Recognise some human processes and explain how these can cause changes in places and environments. ● Recognise how and why people seek to create and manage sustainable environments and to identify opportunities for their own involvement. ● Investigate an environmental issue, caused by change in an environment, ● Identify and explain different views that people, including themselves, hold about topical geographical issues.	Set the scene for the role-play activity. There are plans to build a new landfill site close by. Brainstorm ideas about who the landfill development might affect. In small mixed ability groups, children are given a role-play card from photocopiable page 160. Each group elects a spokesperson to take on the role, supported by the others. In role, children debate the issue. Overall, arguments for and against the building of the landfill site will be voiced. At the end, the whole class votes on the issue. As a class, discuss who has the power to make the decision for or against the issue, and action the children might take to try to influence the decision. Discuss the need to be active citizens who get their voices heard and their views listened to.	● can identify and explain different views that people, including themselves, hold about topical geographical issues. ● know how to influence decision making processes recognise how and why people may seek to create and manage sustainable environments, and can identify opportunities for their own involvement.	Citizenship: everyone has the right to have their opinion listened to and considered

Resources

Access to computers with word-processing and spreadsheet software; access to the Internet; clean rubbish of a variety of different types (washed and dried); dice and coloured counters; local maps at different scales, which include a landfill site; historical maps and aerial photographs of the same area; transport to landfill site; parental permission forms; risk assessment for landfill site visit; First Aid equipment; adult helpers for visit in ratio of 1 to 5 (or as recommended by your LEA); maps of the local area at different scales; items borrowed from your local Development Education Centre (DEC) or elsewhere made by people in less economically developed countries from re-used materials eg toy cars made out of tin cans and wire, sandals made out of old car tyres – borrow photographic evidence as well; photocopiable pages 156–160 (page 157 enlarged and laminated, page 160 copied onto card and cut into role-play cards).

CHAPTER 5
ENVIRONMENTAL
CHANGE

What happens
to all that
waste?

What do we throw away?

What you need and preparation

You will need: a copy of photocopiable page 156 for each child; a lunchtime for data collection; access to computers with spreadsheet software.

What to do

Introduction

10 mins Introduce the lesson, and the unit, by finding out what the children already know about rubbish and waste management. Get the children to undertake a simple baseline assessment, working individually, using the 'concept mapping' idea. Ask each child to write the word 'Rubbish' or 'Waste' in the middle of a sheet of paper and then to brainstorm individual words connected to the subject arranged around the centre. They should join the words to the central concept, and make brief notes along the joining lines to explain the link. They can demonstrate wider knowledge of the subject by linking words to the 'spokes' in the same way.

As a whole class, discuss some of the ideas that evolve from the children's concept maps.

Explain to the children the focus of the lesson:

● to raise issues about the amount of waste we throw away and the consequences of this

● to collect (through fieldwork investigation), record and analyse evidence and draw conclusions

● to recognise that the actions of individuals at a local level can make a difference to global environmental problems and contribute towards sustainable development.

Development

1 hour Explain to the children that they are going to investigate the amount of rubbish that is thrown away in school over one lunchtime. Brainstorm the sort of items the children think may be thrown away during lunchtime, and discuss how to categorise these items and how to collect the information.

Then ask the children, in mixed-ability groups of five or six, to use the information from the brainstorming session and discussion to design a data-collection sheet to help them carry out a simple 'rubbish' survey at lunchtime in school.

During a lunchtime, the children should carry out the survey using their data-collection sheets. Then, in the same mixed-ability groups, the children should record the data collected using a spreadsheet. This may be done on the computer, using a spreadsheet software package. Ask the children to analyse this data, and then to discuss the origins of some of the rubbish and the materials of which it is made.

In the same groups, the children should discuss the data on photocopiable page 156. Then, using this and their own data, consider what actions each one of us could take to reduce the amount of rubbish we produce.

Plenary

5 mins At the end of the lesson, ask each group to contribute some ideas for actions that each one of us could take to reduce the amount of rubbish we produce. Discuss some of the ideas.

Learning objectives

● Recognise how people can improve the environment or damage it.
● Use appropriate geographical vocabulary.
● Collect and record evidence.
● Analyse evidence and draw conclusions.
● Use ICT to help in geographical investigations.
● Recognise how and why people may seek to manage environments sustainably, and to identify opportunities for their own involvement.
● Investigate attempts to manage the environment sustainably.
● Use appropriate fieldwork techniques.

Lesson organisation

Initial teacher-led introduction and simple baseline assessment activity, then whole-class discussion on data collection. Children work in mixed-ability groups of five to six to design a data collection sheet, and then to record (during a lunchtime), present and analyse the data collected. Further group work analysing information on photocopiable page 156, and considering what actions we could all take to reduce the rubbish we produce. Whole-class plenary session at the end.

Vocabulary
plastics
textiles
metals
organic
rubbish
waste

ICT opportunities
Children can use a computer spreadsheet software package for recording, analysing and presenting the 'rubbish' data.

Follow-up activity
Children could collect information about the amount and types of waste their class throws away in a day or a week. This information could be recorded by weight instead of by item; for example, weight of paper, weight of plastic, and so on. The information could be entered into a computer database and the children could make suggestions as to how the class could re-use some of the waste.

Differentiation

The activities in this lesson are open-ended, and therefore support differentiation by outcome. The children work in mixed-ability groups, and so support each other in their work. Use human resources (classroom assistants/voluntary helpers), if available, to work with less able children.

Assessing learning outcomes

Ephemeral evidence

● Observation of, and listening to, the children's discussion as they analyse and present their data.
● Questions asked by the children and answers given to questions framed by the teacher.
● Geographical vocabulary used by the children when undertaking the activity.
● Teamwork and co-operation – how well do the children work together in groups?

Retainable evidence

● Children's initial concept maps.
● Children's data collection sheets.
● Children's data recording, presentation and analysis.

(1 hour) How can we be less wasteful?

Learning objectives
● Recognise how people can improve the environment or damage it.
● Recognise how and why people seek to create and manage sustainable environments and to identify opportunities for their own involvement.
● Investigate attempts to manage the environment sustainably.

Lesson organisation
Initial teacher-led introduction and class discussion about the '4 Rs' of rubbish minimisation, followed by sorting rubbish exercise in mixed ability groups of approximately four to six children. Then, in the same groups, children play the 'Waste not, want not' game (photocopiable page 157). Whole-class plenary session at the end.

What you need and preparation

You will need: clean rubbish of a variety of different types (collected by the class and teacher, and washed and dried); a laminated A3 enlargement of the 'Waste not, want not' game on photocopiable page 157 for each group; dice and coloured counters for each group.

The rules of the 'Waste not, want not' game are similar to those of 'Snakes and Ladders'. Throw a six to start. If you land on a square where there is an action, read the action and either move on, move back or miss turns as instructed. The first to reach 100 is the winner.

What to do

(15 mins) Introduction

Start with a short discussion about the meaning of the phrase 'waste not, want not' and the problems caused by throwing things away. Then introduce children to the '4 Rs' of rubbish minimisation – refuse, re-use, recycle and reduce (see 'Background information' on page 100). Discuss what the four rules mean.

CHAPTER 5
ENVIRONMENTAL
CHANGE

What happens
to all that
waste?

Explain to the children the focus of the lesson:
● to raise issues about the amounts of waste we throw away and the consequences of this
● to develop children's knowledge and understanding of waste minimisation and waste management
● to recognise that actions of individuals at a local level can make a difference to global environmental problems and contribute towards sustainable development
● to raise issues about the amounts of valuable raw materials and energy wasted through throwing all types of waste into the refuse bin.

Vocabulary
refuse
reduce
recycle
re-use
repair
compost
waste minimisation
waste management

(40 mins) Development

Provide each mixed-ability group of four to six children (depending on the size of the class) with half a bin or sack full of a variety of clean rubbish (collected by the class and teacher from home, and washed and dried carefully before the lesson). The items should be made of different materials such as glass, paper, polystyrene, wood, plastic, aluminium, steel, cellophane and vegetable matter.

Ask the children to sift through the rubbish, sorting it into piles of items that you can re-use or repair, compost, recycle, reduce, and other items that cannot be re-used or recycled in any way. They should discuss the benefits or costs of each method towards the environment, and record their decisions on a large table, using headings as illustrated below:

Re-use/Repair	Compost	Recycle	Reduce (minimise)	Other

In the same mixed-ability groups, children then play the 'Waste not, want not' game using the game board on photocopiable page 157. In their groups, they should discuss the penalties and bonuses for undertaking certain actions when landing on some squares.

(5 mins) Plenary

At the end of the lesson, as a class, discuss the game and what the children have learned about waste minimisation from the two activities.

ICT opportunities
Children could use ICT to record and present the data from their rubbish sorting activity.

Follow-up activities
● Children could write a poem or rap about the '4 Rs' of rubbish minimisation – refuse, re-use, recycle, reduce.
● Children could use the Internet and other reference sources to find out about how glass or paper are recycled.

Differentiation

Children work in mixed-ability groups and so support each other. The 'Waste not, want not' game is accessible to all, regardless of ability, and so encourages all children to be actively involved.

Less able children may benefit from working with classroom assistants or voluntary helpers, if available.

More able children could locate recycling centres for glass, aluminium and paper, textile banks, charity shops and second-hand outlets, household waste disposal centres, landfill sites, waste incinerators and other features associated with waste management, and record them on a map of the local area.

Assessing learning outcomes

Ephemeral evidence

● Observation of, and listening to, the children's discussion as they sort the rubbish and play the game.

● Questions asked by the children and answers given to questions framed by the teacher.

● Geographical vocabulary used by the children when undertaking the activities.

● Teamwork and co-operation – how well do the children work together in groups?

Retainable evidence

● Children's tables of results from the group sorting activity.

4-5 hours What happens at a landfill site?

Learning objectives
● Recognise how people can improve the environment or damage it.
● Recognise how and why people seek to create and manage sustainable environments and to identify opportunities for their own involvement.
● Investigate attempts to manage the environment sustainably.
● Use appropriate fieldwork techniques.

What you need and preparation

You will need: local maps at different scales which include the landfill site; historical maps if appropriate (available from libraries and record offices); aerial photographs of the area in which the landfill site is located; transport to the landfill site; parental permission forms; risk assessment; First Aid equipment; adult helpers in the ratio of 1:5 (or as recommended by your LEA); a copy of photocopiable page 158 for each child.

What to do

10 mins Introduction

As a class, discuss what a landfill site is (see 'Background information' on page 100). Discuss aspects of health and safety involved in the proposed visit to a landfill site. (If possible, arrange for a member of staff from the site to come into school before the

CHAPTER 5
ENVIRONMENTAL
CHANGE

What happens
to all that
waste?

visit to talk to the children about health and safety.) Draw up a set of health and safety rules to be applied on the visit.

Explain to the children the focus of the lesson:

● to carry out fieldwork investigations at a landfill site, and use appropriate field techniques to find out what happens there

● to raise issues about the amount of waste we throw away and the consequences of this

● to develop children's knowledge and understanding of waste management.

 4 hours **Development**
Part 1: classroom-based activity – locating the landfill site (45 minutes)

● In mixed-ability groups of five or six, the children locate the local landfill site on maps and on aerial photographs. They should give four- or six-figure grid references for the site. If possible, children should look at historical maps of the same area, and see what was there before the landfill site.

● In groups, children plan the best route to the landfill site from the school. They should discuss what the criteria for the 'best route' should be.

● As a class, discuss the suggested routes to the landfill site. Are all the routes the same? If not, why not? What decisions have the different groups taken?

Part 2: field-based activity – visit to the landfill site (about 3 hours)

● Visit the landfill site. Make sure the children know why they are visiting the site (to see how much rubbish is produced and what happens to it), what to look for (see below), and the questions to ask (for example, What kind of rubbish can/can't you put in a landfill site? Why is this a good place for a landfill site? What do local residents think? How long will it take to fill up? What happens to it then?). Ensure all health and safety procedures are followed.

● During the site visit, children should find out how the cells (separate pits or hollows, which together make up the landfill site) are made and filled in, any effects the site has on the local community, and how the land is returned to fields, forests and walks after the cells are filled. If possible, they should see a cell currently being used, a cell under construction and a cell being returned to community use. They should observe machines working and visit the wheel-wash and the weighbridge.

Part 3: classroom-based activity – writing reports (30 minutes)

● As a whole class, briefly discuss the visit to the landfill site.

● Working individually, children should then write up a report of the visit to the landfill site using the writing frame on photocopiable page 158. Their written work could be displayed in a large dustbin-shaped book.

10 mins **Plenary**
As a whole class, discuss children's views about the landfill site. What did they learn? What surprised them? What do they want to find out more about?

Differentiation

Less able children could use a word bank of useful vocabulary (provided by the teacher) to help them write about their visit.

Lesson organisation
Initial teacher-led introduction on health and safety aspects of a visit to a landfill site. In mixed-ability groups of five to six, children locate the landfill site on a map and plan the best route to take from the school. Whole-class discussion after the visit, after which children produce individual reports about the visit. Whole-class plenary at the end on children's reactions to the landfill site, and what they learned.

Vocabulary
landfill
topsoil
sub-soil
clay
incineration
methane gas
leachate
run-off
toxic waste
cells
clay
geology

What happens to all that waste?

Use human resources (classroom assistants/voluntary helpers), if available, to work with less able children.

More able children could write interviews with imaginary characters or machines they saw at the landfill site; for example, Carl Compacter, Laura Landfill, Walter Weigh Bridge, William Wheel Wash, Scientific Sarah (Science Officer), Elaine the Engineer, Earth Worm Edward. Working in groups, they could put the interviews together to make a news programme called 'Waste Watch UK', and present it to the rest of the class or possibly the rest of the school. (This may replace writing an account of the visit.)

Assessing learning outcomes
Ephemeral evidence
● Observation of, and listening to, the children's discussion as they prepare for, and then go on, the visit.
● Questions asked by the children and answers given to questions framed by the teacher.
● Geographical vocabulary used by the children when undertaking the activities.
● Teamwork and co-operation – how well do the children work together in groups?
Retainable evidence
● Children's accounts of the visit to landfill site, including copies of photocopiable page 158.

① What do other people do with their rubbish?
1 hour

What you need and preparation
From your local Development Education Centre (DEC), or other appropriate sources, borrow items made by people in different less economically developed countries from re-used materials; borrow photographic evidence as well. Some suggestions of artefacts or photographs to borrow are listed below – there are many other examples:
● Toys, especially cars made out of tin cans and wire (from Africa or South America, for example)
● Sandals made out of old car tyres (for example, Kenya)
● Spinning wheels made out of old bicycle wheels (for example, India)
● Cooking pots and spoons made from recycled aluminium tins and car parts (for example, Kenya, Ghana)
● Inner tubes from car tyres made into water bags (for example, Kenya)
● Household products made out of tin cans – buckets and barrels for water, vegetable cutters (India), funnels, paraffin lamps, charcoal stoves, cocoa pod cutter (Ghana), sieves (Columbia).

You will need: a copy of photocopiable page 159 for each child in the class to complete.

What to do
Introduction
10 mins
Recap and discuss methods of re-using and recycling waste in the UK. Discuss how some people, particularly in less economically developed countries, make their living by sorting through waste looking for items to recycle or re-use (see 'Background information' on page 100). Brainstorm and discuss the dangers and problems of this type of lifestyle, as well as the benefits. Explain to the children about the artefacts you have for them to look at.

CHAPTER 5
ENVIRONMENTAL
CHANGE

What happens
to all that
waste?

Explain to the children the focus of the lesson:
● to raise issues about how waste can be re-used and the creativity and resourcefulness of some people in less economically developed countries
● to raise issues about the dangers of making a living from scavenging rubbish tips.

40 mins Development
Give five or six artefacts and photographs of articles made from recycled materials from different countries to each mixed-ability group of five or six children. Allow the children to handle and discuss each article.

In their groups, the children should select three articles. For each article, they should discuss what it is, how it has been made and by whom, and for what it is used. Working individually within the group, each child should complete photocopiable page 159. In groups, they should locate the country of origin of each of the recycled items on a world map or globe.

In small groups or pairs, the children should design and make clothes out of waste products. Later, they could present a 'Waste Clothes Show', describing the outfit each model is wearing and for what occasion the outfit has been designed. The event could be photographed to add realism and to provide evidence for assessment.

10 mins Plenary
At the end of the lesson, discuss what the children found out about recycling in less economically developed countries.

Differentiation
This is an open-ended activity, to which children of all abilities have equal access – they are able to work at their own level.

Less able children may benefit from working with classroom assistants or voluntary helpers, if available.

More able children could select one country where recycling is a way of life and find out all they can about those involved in that recycling. They should then report back to the class.

Assessing learning outcomes
Ephemeral evidence
● Observation of, and listening to, the children's discussion as they look at the artefacts.
● Questions asked by the children and answers given to questions framed by the teacher.
● Geographical vocabulary used by the children when undertaking the activities.
● Teamwork and co-operation – how well do the children work together in groups and pairs?
Retainable evidence
● Children's completed photocopiable page 159.
● Photographic evidence of the 'Waste Clothes Show'.

Vocabulary
recycle
rag trade
street children
disease
danger
contaminated

ICT opportunities
Children could use the Internet to find out more about the problems faced by people who make a living from rubbish tips.

Follow-up activity
Children could take part in the 'Paper Bag Game' (developed by Christian Aid). In Calcutta, India, some very poor families live on the pavements, because they cannot afford rent even for one-room shacks. The children make paper bags out of waste to sell for money. The game takes an hour to play, and involves children making paper bags for which they are paid at the same rates as the children in Calcutta, and then seeing if they can pay the rent and buy enough food to live on. Contact Christian Aid for further details of this activity.

CHAPTER 5
ENVIRONMENTAL
CHANGE

What happens
to all that
waste?

Where shall we build a new landfill site?
(1 hour)

Learning objectives
● Recognise how people can improve the environment or damage it, and how decisions about places and environments affect the future quality of people's lives.
● Recognise some human processes and explain how these can cause changes in places and environments.
● Recognise how and why people seek to create and manage sustainable environments and to identify opportunities for their own involvement.
● Investigate an environmental issue, caused by change in an environment, and attempts to manage the environment sustainably.
● Investigate an issue arising from changes in land-use
● Identify and explain different views that people, including themselves, hold about topical geographical issues.

Lesson organisation
Teacher-led introduction to set the scene for the role-play activity, followed by simple brainstorming activity. Mixed-ability group work (two or three children) based on a role-play activity, followed by whole-class discussion on how to be responsible, active citizens. Whole-class plenary session discussing the types of actions the children could undertake to try to influence the decision-making processes involved in the location of a new landfill site.

Vocabulary
landfill
development
traffic
census
environmental
impact

What you need and preparation
You will need: the role-play cards from photocopiable page 160, copied on to card, cut up and issued one card to each group of children; maps of the local area at different scales.

What to do

Introduction
(10 mins) Introduce the lesson by setting the scene for the role-play activity; there are plans to build a new landfill site close by.

Explain to the children the focus of the lesson:
● raise issues about the amount of land required for landfill
● raise issues about land-use and its impact on local communities
● raise issues about the amounts of waste we throw away and the consequences of this
● understand that children have a right to have their views and opinions listened to.

Brainstorm ideas about who the landfill development might affect and discuss how these people might be affected.

Development
(45 mins) Split the class into about twelve mixed-ability groups of two or three children. Give each group a role-play card from photocopiable page 160. Ask the children to read their role-play card. Each group is to elect a spokesperson and he or she must take on the role described on the card, supported by the others in the group. In their roles, the children should debate the issue – each group should take a turn to say what they think (through the spokesperson). Overall, arguments for and against the building of a landfill site in the local area will be voiced. At the end of the debate, the whole class should vote on the issue.

As a whole class, discuss who can influence decisions such as the location of a landfill site (the 'stakeholders' – anyone with an interest in the effects of the development), who has the power to make the decision for or against the issue, and what sort of action the children might become involved in to try to influence the decision. For example, they might become involved in collecting, analysing and presenting data from evidence they collect relating to the issue; finding out the opinions of others through questionnaires and debates; putting forward a case in a rational, informed manner; writing letters in the persuasive or discussion genre to people who have the power to make changes; drawing up petitions; making posters; informing people about the opinions of those affected by the issue; contacting media such as the local press; inviting local MPs or councillors in to school, and so on. Discuss with the children the need to be active citizens – not just well-informed individuals, but people who get their voices heard and their views listened to. (See 'Background information' on page 100.)

Plenary
(5 mins) At the end of the lesson, discuss with the children how they would try to influence the decision-making process regarding the building of a landfill site in the local area.

CHAPTER 5
ENVIRONMENTAL
CHANGE

What happens
to all that
waste?

Differentiation

This lesson is open-ended and accessible to all, regardless of ability and so encourages all children to be actively involved.

Less able children may benefit from working with classroom assistants or voluntary helpers, if available.

More able children could write a newspaper article under the headline 'Residents in uproar as local area becomes waste dump for whole region!'

Assessing learning outcomes

Ephemeral evidence

- Observation of, and listening to, the children's discussion as they prepare for and carry out the role-play activity.
- Questions asked by the children and answers given to questions framed by the teacher.
- Geographical vocabulary used by the children when undertaking the activity.
- Teamwork and co-operation – how well do the children work together in groups?

ICT opportunities
The children could use the Internet to find out about the regulations that control the development and use of landfill sites in the UK.

Follow-up activity
Is there a real issue in the children's own locality that they feel strongly about? If so, investigate, and encourage the children to be actively involved. Ask people with information – for example, planners, architects, local councillors – to come in to school to talk through the issue with the children.

PHOTOCOPIABLE

UK LOCALITIES: **The local area**
Where are we? Page 12

Name _____   Date _____

Scaling up! 1

LOCAL

Using an Ordnance Survey map, find your local area and give the six-figure grid reference for the nearest:

church   _____

phone box   _____

school   _____

public house   _____

REGIONAL

Where is your settlement in the UK?
Using an Ordnance Survey map, find your settlement and give the six-figure grid reference for the nearest:

motorway junction   _____

river feature   _____

village   _____

town   _____

city   _____

NATIONAL

Using a UK atlas, find your settlement and name the nearest:

county   _____

conurbation   _____

country   _____

How far is it to:

the nearest airport?   _____

the nearest rail station? _____

London?   _____

Name _____   Date _____

Scaling up! 2

EUROPEAN

Using an atlas of the world, find out the names of the countries that make up the European Union. Label them on this map, and shade your country red.

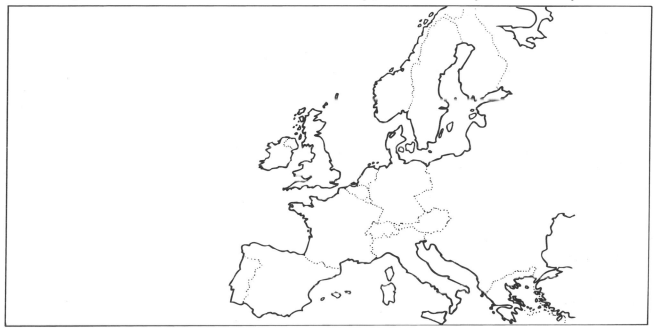

GLOBAL

Using a globe, find out the names of the different continents in the world. Label them on this map, and shade your continent red.

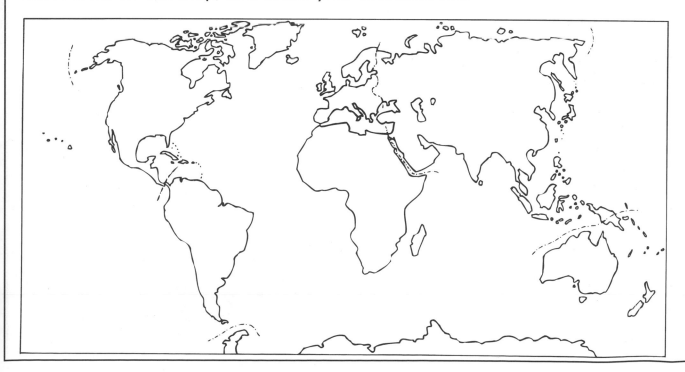

PHOTOCOPIABLE

UK LOCALITIES: **The local area**
What is our settlement like? Page 14

Name _____ Date _____

Detective's report

Historical source	What does it tell me?

Questions I still have to answer:

'Shopping list' of sources I need to answer these questions:

UK LOCALITIES: **The local area**
What is our settlement like? Page 14

PHOTOCOPIABLE

Name _____   Date _____

Our settlement

Use this grid to draw the shape of your settlement, from a photograph. Colour in areas of different land-use in different colours.

Land-use key:

☐ _____   ☐ _____

☐ _____   ☐ _____

UK LOCALITIES: The local area
How do different activities affect our settlement? Page 16

PHOTOCOPIABLE

Name _____ Date _____

Survey of places in the local area

Place: _____

How does it look? Draw sketches and write notes in this space to show how the place looks.	Put a circle around the one that you most agree with. looks awful (**scores 1**) looks OK (**scores 2**) looks nice (**scores 3**)
How does it sound? Is there noise pollution? Draw sketches and write notes in this space to describe what sounds you can hear.	Put a circle around the one that you most agree with. noisy (**scores 1**) not too noisy (**scores 2**) quiet (**scores 3**)
Is there any other pollution? Draw sketches and write notes in this space to describe any evidence of pollution you can see (eg rubbish, graffiti, dead plants or animals).	Put a circle around the one that you most agree with. lots of evidence of pollution (**scores 1**) little evidence of pollution (**scores 2**) no evidence of pollution (**scores 3**)

The **total score** for this place is: _____

UK LOCALITIES: **Contrasting localities**
How does this city compare with our local settlement? Page 21

PHOTOCOPIABLE

Name _____   Date _____

In the city

You have a set of photographs that were taken on a journey through the city.

1 Put the photographs in order, starting at the edge of the city and moving to the centre.

2 When you have done this, use the diagram below to record the main land-uses shown by the pictures.

3 Shade different land-uses using different coloured pencils, and complete the land-use key.

4 Write in the positions of any particular features, such as 'cathedral' or 'river'.

edge of city | | | | | | city centre

Land-use key:

☐ This colour shows _____
☐ This colour shows _____
☐ This colour shows _____

☐ This colour shows _____
☐ This colour shows _____
☐ This colour shows _____

5 (a) What land-uses are near the edge of the city? _____

(b) Why are these activities at the edge and not in the centre? _____

6 (a) What land-uses are near the centre of the city? _____

(b) Why are these activities in the centre and not at the edge? _____

7 (a) How is the pattern of land-use in this city similar to the pattern in your settlement? _____

(b) How is the pattern of land-use different to the pattern in your settlement? _____

PHOTOCOPIABLE

UK LOCALITIES: **Contrasting localities**
How does this town compare with our settlement? Page 23

Name _____   Date _____

Why is this town here?

Look at the town you are studying on an Ordnance Survey map.
● Look at the shape of the land and other physical features.
● Look at the transport links running through the town or close to it.
● Look at the distances to other towns or important places.
● Think about how all these things affect the way the town has grown.
Now draw a plan of the town in the space below. Only include features that
you think help to explain why the town is like it is.

Use this checklist to make sure you've looked at everything.
I have considered:
❏ the shape of the land   ❏ other physical features
❏ where this place is in relation   ❏ transport networks
   to other places   ❏ other human features

Try to use Ordnance Survey symbols to show the features.
Symbols key:
____ This symbol means _____ ____ This symbol means _____
____ This symbol means _____ ____ This symbol means _____
____ This symbol means _____ ____ This symbol means _____

Try to explain why this town is here.

This town is expanding/declining. Why do you think this is?

UK LOCALITIES: **Contrasting localities**
How does this hamlet compare with our local area? Page 27

PHOTOCOPIABLE

Name _____   Date _____

What's in a hamlet? What's in a village?

What will your hamlet need to become a village?

Choose from the following features:

Name _____   Date _____

Finding out about India

Using all the resources available, find out some information about India. Write down what you find out on this page, and on the other side if you run out of space.

	Atlases and maps	Books, CD-ROMs	Photographs	Internet
Population and size of India				
Flag				
Currency and exchange rate				
Major religions of India				
Source and length of two major Indian rivers				
Languages and dialects – what are the official languages?				
Four major cities and their population data				
Climatic data for India (record this on the back of this page)				
Farming – variety of crops produced				
Food				
Industries – what goods are manufactured in India?				
Where is India's film industry based?				

● Which source of information was the easiest to use? Why?
● Which source of information was the most up-to-date?
● Did each of the sources give the same information in the same form? How easy was it to compare?

ECONOMICALLY DEVELOPING COUNTRIES: India – a land of many contrasts
What is the climate like in India? Page 33

PHOTOCOPIABLE

Name _____   Date _____

Climate data for Bangalore

	Jan	Feb	Mar	Apr	May	Jun	Jul	Aug	Sep	Oct	Nov	Dec
Temp (°C)	24	25	27	28	30	29	28	27	27	28	27	25
Rainfall (mm)	0	1	0	0	20	647	945	660	309	117	7	1

(Data taken from *Bangalore: Indian City Life*, from ActionAid)

1 Pretend you are a reporter for the *Indian Daily Star*, a national newspaper. Write a weather report for Bangalore for 10th July. Make some notes in the space below. Include a local map in your report and an interview with a local rice farmer. How does the farmer feel now the monsoon has arrived?

2 You are going to visit a friend in Bangalore in early July. What sort of clothes must you pack and why?

3 If you visited your friend in December, how would what you pack be different?

PHOTOCOPIABLE

ECONOMICALLY DEVELOPING COUNTRIES: India – a land of many contrast
What is life like for children in India? Page 34

Name _____   Date _____

Wants and needs – basic rights

In your group, make lists of things that people want and things that people need. Write these headings on a separate sheet and use them to make your lists.

Wants	Needs

In your group, discuss these questions:
● What are the differences between wants and needs?
● Do wants and needs differ for different people?
● Would the wants and needs of children in India be the same as your own? Explain your reasons.

The most basic needs are called **rights**.
Rights are things that it is fair and just for a person to have or to be able to do.

In your group, discuss the things you have written under the 'needs' heading. Decide on six of these needs that you think are the most important needs for all children. Make a new list of these six **basic rights**.

Read about the lives of Madhan and Badichi, then answer the following questions on a separate sheet:
1 (a) Where do Madhan and Badichi live?
  (b) Locate their home village of Chembakolli on a map of India.
2 (a) Do Madhan and Badichi have access to clean, safe drinking water?
  (b) Where does the water come from?
  (c) How do they get the water?
3 (a) Do Madhan and Badichi have enough to eat?
  (b) What do they eat?
4 (a) Do Madhan and Badichi go to school?
  (b) Describe the type of education they receive.
5 (a) What kind of healthcare do Madhan and Badichi receive?
  (b) Have they been vaccinated?
  (c) Do they have a health centre to go to when they are sick?
6 What would you like about their lifestyle? What would you find difficult?
7 Do you think Madhan and Badichi's basic rights are being met?
Answer the same questions for each of the other children – Penchi, Babu and Khushboo.

Name _____ Date _____

Meet the children

Madhan is 7 years old. He lives with his grandparents and his older sister, Badichi (10 years old) in a small village called Chembakolli. Some of Madhan's other relatives live next door and both Madhan and Badichi help with household chores. Madhan's sister, Badichi gets up at 5.30am each day and goes with her aunt to collect water from the well. It takes over an hour as the water is very heavy to carry, and the return journey is all uphill. Madhan's relatives work on the land, growing tea, peppers and vegetables. Madhan helps them with all the farm work. The daily income for the family of seven is 120 rupees (£1.70). Madhan's sister, Badichi, looks after her little cousins, their little brother and their grandparents during the day. She also sweeps the floor of the house and helps prepare the meals for all the family. Both children help collect the firewood for the fire. Madhan's family do not have much money and have little education. Two of Madhan's cousins go to school but he and his sister do not. If any of the family is ill, they visit the tribal health centre in the next village of Kanjikolly. Here, treatment is cheap, otherwise they could not afford to pay for it.

Penchi (11 years old) and his sister Patma (9) live in Bangalore. Penchi's father makes gold jewellery and his mother teaches English. They live in a three-roomed house with an outside tap. The children go to a private school from 8am until 1pm. They study English, maths, science and citizenship. In his spare time, Penchi likes to play chess and cricket. Patma is learning traditional Indian dances. The weekly family income is about 1750 rupees (£31). The children have lovely meals, cooked by a housemaid, and are never hungry. They like to watch television at night and often go to the cinema. They have no routine chores to do, just general help around the house.

Babu is 12 years old. He lives in Calcutta. He is an orphan and has no mother or father. Babu is a 'street child'. He has no fixed home, sleeps on the street and earns a very poor living from collecting waste to be recycled and sometimes shining shoes. Babu has never been to school. He cannot read or write and is often bullied by older boys on the street. Babu often goes without food for several days. Babu has also had to steal from others so he could eat.

Khushboo is 12 years old and lives in New Delhi. When she was 10, her father became ill and was unable to work. He borrowed money (a loan) from a rich man and in repayment the rich man was given Khushboo. She has to work to pay off the loan and also the interest on the loan. She is bonded to the rich man's family. Khushboo's labour is valued at 50 rupees (80p) per month, because the rich man's family feeds and clothes her. Khushboo does all the housework and looks after

the rich man's children. She has no free time and is never allowed to visit her family. Khushboo's life is very hard. She sees all the advantages the rich man's children have (education, time to play, good food, good healthcare, lovely clothes and a comfortable home to live in), but has none of these herself.

PHOTOCOPIABLE

ECONOMICALLY DEVELOPING COUNTRIES: India – a land of many contrast
How do people travel in India? Page 36

Name _____   Date _____

Transport and sustainability

Look at each type of transport shown in the photographs. Tick the boxes to show where people use this type of transport.

	India – rural transport	India – urban transport	UK – rural transport	UK – urban transport
Bicycle				
Cart pulled by tractor				
Cart pulled by ox, horse or camel				
Motor car				
Train				
Buses and coaches				
Tram				
Rickshaw (Pedal-powered)				
Rickshaw (Motorised)				
Walking				
Scooters				
Aeroplane				

Answer these questions on a separate sheet of paper:

1 What fuel powers each type of transport?
2 Which fuel is most environmentally friendly?
3 Which type of transport are you most likely to use, and least likely to use?
4 How do you think Madhan and Badichi, Penchi, Babu, and Khushboo travel around?
5 Most people in India use public transport, and most people in the UK use private transport. Why do you think this is?
6 How might transport in India change in the future?

ECONOMICALLY DEVELOPING COUNTRIES: India – a land of many contrasts

What do people eat in India? Page 37

PHOTOCOPIABLE

Name _____   Date _____

Investigating Indian artefacts

What do you think your artefact is called?

Main things to think about	Further questions	Things found out through looking and handling	Things to be researched
PHYSICAL FEATURES What does it look and feel like?	What colour is it? What does it smell like? What sound does it make? What is it made of? Is it a natural or artificial substance? Has it been altered, adapted, mended? Can it be worn?		
CONSTRUCTION How is it made?	Is it handmade or machine-made? Was it made in a mould or in pieces? How has it been fixed together?		
FUNCTION What is it made for?	How is the object used?		
DESIGN Is it well designed?	What is it used for? Does it do the job it was intended for well? Were the best materials available for the job used? Is it decorated? Do you like the way it looks?		
VALUE What is it worth?	What is it worth to the people who made it? What is it worth to the people who use it?		

PHOTOCOPIABLE

Name _____   Date _____

The River Nile from source to mouth

1 Using your atlas and other maps, locate and label the following on this map:

Source of the River Nile
Blue Nile
Mouth of the River Nile
Mediterranean sea
Delta
Red Sea
Lake Victoria
Suez Canal
Aswan Dam
Sahara Desert
Lake Nasser
Cairo
White Nile
Alexandria

2 Where is the source of the River Nile?
3 Which sea does the River Nile flow into?
4 What are the names of two of the tributaries of the River Nile?
5 What compass direction does the water flow in?

ECONOMICALLY DEVELOPING COUNTRIES: Egypt – a land of surprises
How do the Egyptians control the waters of the River Nile? Page 43

PHOTOCOPIABLE

Name _____   Date _____

Aswan Dam – good or bad?

The dam produces enough electricity for every village, town and city in Egypt.	Lake Nasser provides recreational facilities. It is also a good place to watch wildlife.	The wildlife and ecology of the river has been affected by the dam.	Neighbouring countries, upstream from the Dam, could divert the course of the Nile.
It is now possible to have more than one harvest each year.	The Egyptians are very proud to have the largest dam in the world and the largest artificial lake.	Water-borne diseases such as typhoid are spreading more rapidly than before, because the river and the canals never dry out completely.	There is the danger of an earthquake because of the great weight of the water in the lake and its proximity to a geological fault line.
The stored water allows more land to be irrigated and so more crops can be grown.	The dam allows more crops to be grown, so there are more jobs for people in the rural areas.	More than 120 000 people had to leave their homes and be resettled in other areas to provide the land to flood to create Lake Nasser.	Fish numbers are diminishing because artificial fertilisers run off the land and into the river and lake and poison the fish.
Many archaeological sights – temples, tombs etc – were moved or lost under the water. The increase in salt levels caused erosion and crumbling to those that were moved.	Floods no longer threaten the villages and towns.	The dam stopped the seasonal flooding, and so the fertile silt deposits stopped. Farmers now have to buy expensive fertilisers to help their crops grow.	The Nile flows more slowly into the sea because of the dam. So salt water from the sea flows back up the Delta and increases the salt levels in the soil, making it barren and useless.
There is no longer the threat of drought every year.	Large-scale heavy industry has grown up around the dam.	Electricity is cheap.	There is a risk the dam could be bombed.

PHOTOCOPIABLE

ECONOMICALLY DEVELOPING COUNTRIES: Egypt – a land of surprises
How do the Egyptians control the waters of the Nile? Page 43

Name _____   Date _____

Aswan Dam – a good thing for Egypt or a big mistake?

What do *you* think?
Using the statements on the cards your teacher has given you, discuss the positive benefits and negative effects the Aswan Dam has on the physical landscape, people and economy of the Nile Valley.
Select statements to put forward both sides of the argument.

The question we are discussing is

The positive benefits of the Aswan Dam are

The negative effects of the Aswan Dam are

After looking at both sides of the discussion, I think that

This evidence supports my view

ECONOMICALLY DEVELOPING COUNTRIES: Egypt – a land of surprises
Why is the River Nile important for tourism? Page 45

PHOTOCOPIABLE

Name _____   Date _____

Eight activities for a cruise on the Nile

Names of members of group:

_____

_____

Activity
1

Activity
2

Activity
3

Activity
4

Activity
5

Activity
6

Activity
7

Activity
8

PHOTOCOPIABLE

ECONOMICALLY DEVELOPING COUNTRIES: Egypt – a land of surprises
What kind of settlements are on the banks of the Nile? Page 47

Name _____   Date _____

Fact file

Name of settlement: _____
Type of settlement: _____
Location of settlement: _____

People (families, occupations, roles played in family and so on)	
Houses and homes (types of houses found within the settlement)	
Schools and education	
Food and meals	
Farming/agriculture (what is produced and who will use the produce)	
Industry	
Tourist trade	
Transport	
Shops and markets	
Leisure activities	
Any environmental concerns/issues	

Settlement survey

Name of settlement: _____

Look at the photographs of the settlement you are studying.
In the table below, colour the circles next to the words that best
describe your settlement. Add your own words to the lists if you
need to.

Landscape
○ valley
○ hill
○ river
○ slope
○ cliffs
○ desert
○ lake
○ sea
○ oasis
○ scrubland

Buildings
○ religious building
○ factory
○ farm
○ hotel
○ modern houses
○ older houses
○ craft workshop
○ shops
○ school

Transport
○ car
○ bus
○ train
○ bike
○ camel
○ donkey
○ lorry
○ tractor
○ motorbike
○ tractor
○ walking

Land-use
○ farming
○ industry
○ housing
○ playground
○ wasteland
○ desert
○ gardens
○ tourism

Environment
○ attractive
○ clean
○ dirty
○ interesting
○ noisy
○ quiet
○ smelly
○ ugly
○ untidy
○ dull

Name _____   Date _____

River snap

river		meander	
source		estuary	
tributary		ox bow lake	
confluence		delta	
waterfall		mouth	

Name _____   Date _____

River features

Add labels to this diagram to name all the river features.

Name _____   Date _____

Down the river

Aerial photograph: _____
In each box, record what you can find out about the river at the place this
aerial photograph shows.

What physical features can you see?

What human features can you see?

What is the land around the river used for?

How do you feel about this area? What is the river like here?

Who uses the river? What is the river used for?

Map
Now look at the map for the same area.
Locate the position of the aerial photograph using grid references or
co-ordinates.

Grid references: _____

Find the features you found on the aerial photograph on the map.
Does the map give you any more information about the area?
Add this to the boxes above.

PHOTOCOPIABLE

Name _____   Date _____

River game 1

1 START RIVER SOURCE, IN UPLAND AREA

2

3 Torrential rainfall, water runs off the land, washing away soil and plants. **Miss a turn.**

4

5 Little rainfall this year. **Go back to the start.**

6

7 Steep slopes, fast-flowing streams. **Go on to 12.**

8

9

10

11 Fast water erodes the bank on the outside of a meander and causes a landslide. **Go back to 9.**

12

13 Waterfall increases the energy of the stream. **Go on to 22.**

14 Increase in volume of water due to increase in number of tributaries. **Go on to 22.**

15 A small tributary of the river is studied by school children. **Move on 2 places.**

16 Environmental indicators, found by school children in a study, indicate the tributary is very clean. **Move on 4 places.**

17

18 Reservoir built in flooded valley, homes and wildlife habitats destroyed. **Miss a turn.**

19 Reservoir built, which controls the water, stores water for future use and prevents flooding. **Move on 3 places.**

20

21 Reservoir used for recreational use. **Go on to 24.**

22

23 Conflict of use of river: farming, forestry and leisure. **Miss a turn.**

24

25

26 Water pumped out of river to irrigate farmland. **Go back to 17.**

27

28

29

30

31 Angling club use river for competition fishing. **Move on 2 places.**

32

33

34 River narrows under a bridge, water rushes through. **Go on to 39.**

35

36

37 River polluted by farmyard slurry, life in river killed – angling club can no longer use the river. **Miss a turn.**

38

39

40

41 River slows on the inside of a meander. **Go back to 35.**

42

43

44

45

46 New houses built – water removed for domestic uses. **Miss a turn.**

47

48

49

50

Name _____   Date _____

River game 2

51	70	71 Reservoir used for recreational use. **Go on to 74.**	90 Docks no longer used. **Miss a turn.**	91 New ferry terminal developed. **Move on 3 places.**
52 Riverside walk and environmental area constructed by local council. **Move on 4 places.**	69	72 Sewage is dumped in river. **Miss 2 goes.**	89 Docks pump out water to float a ship. **Go back to 79.**	92
53	68 Old industrial site redeveloped into apartments. **Move on 2 places.**	73	88	93 Beech found to be polluted and does not receive European flag. **Miss 2 turns.**
54	67	74	87	94
55	66 Water warmed by industrial processes, leads to increased trout breeding, but water is able to hold less oxygen. **Miss a turn.**	75	86 New tourist dockside development, improving the environment. **Move on to 92.**	95 Environmental quality of beach and water improved. **Move on to 98.**
56	65	76 Education centre open for all schools to use. **Move on 4 places.**	85	96
57 Household rubbish, supermarket trolleys, old mattresses dumped in river. **Miss a go.**	64 Water polluted by industrial waste. **Throw a 6 to move on.**	77	84	97 Mud flats slow the rate of flow to the sea. **Go back 3 places.**
58	63	78	83	98
59	62	79 River tidal to this point – incoming tide slows the river. **Miss a turn.**	82	99 Water polluted by spillage from oil tanker – wildlife is affected. **Go back to 56 and miss a turn.**
60	61 Local school children spend their holidays, with adults, cleaning up the river. **Move to 65.**	80	81	100 **FINISH MOUTH OF RIVER, AT THE SEA**

PHOTOCOPIABLE

WATER AND ITS EFFECTS ON THE LANDSCAPE: Rivers
What causes river pollution? Page 57

Name _____   Date _____

What a load of rubbish!

1 Look at the following rubbish found in streams. Tick a box to show how dangerous you think each type of rubbish is. Then, in the last column, write why you think this.

Type of rubbish	Very dangerous	Slightly dangerous	Not at all dangerous	Reasons for my answer
empty cans and beer bottles				
rusty supermarket trolleys, old bicycles				
leaves				
old mattresses				
car tyres				
twigs and branches				
oil, petrol and diesel cans				
crisp and sweet packets				
broken glass				
aerosols and canisters				
packing straps				
polystyrene and plastic packaging				

2 Can you think of any other rubbish sometimes found in rivers and streams?

_____

3 Write down ways in which some of this rubbish can be dangerous to:
● a small child _____
● a cat _____
● a duck _____

4 Write an article for your local newspaper, telling them about the problem of rubbish in the river.
5 Draw a picture of a river. Put ten pieces of rubbish in your picture and ask a friend to identify the ten pieces of rubbish.

PRIMARY FOUNDATIONS: Geography: Ages 9–11

WATER AND ITS EFFECTS ON THE LANDSCAPE: Rivers
How do rivers shape the landscape? Page 59

PHOTOCOPIABLE

Name _____   Date _____

The work of a river

1 What causes rivers to have energy?

_____

2 How do rivers use the energy they have?

_____

3 What word means 'wear away'?

_____

Erosion

A river wears away the rocks along the river bed using many tools – it dissolves rock away, it uses pebbles, gravel and sand as if they were sandpaper, and it uses the actual force of the water.

4 Find out what these terms mean. Write your findings here.

Corrasion _____

Attrition _____

Abrasion or scouring _____

Corrosion _____

Hydraulic action _____

Transportation

5 Rivers carry materials in different ways. Draw a line from each method of transportation to the right place in the diagram below.

Solution (invisible or dissolved rock in the water)

Traction (large boulders and pebbles are rolled along the riverbed)

Suspended load (silt and mud suspended)

Saltation (sand hops, bounces and skips along the river bed)

Deposition

6 Describe when and why a river deposits its load.

_____

_____

Add words about the work of a river to your glossary.

WATER AND ITS EFFECTS ON THE LANDSCAPE: **Coasts**

PHOTOCOPIABLE   *What does this coastline look like? Page 63*

Name _____   Date _____

Coastal features

Look at the six photographs showing coastal environments.

In your group, talk about how these places are similar. Talk about how they are different. Think about the different human and physical features you can see, and the ways they were made.

Now fill in this table to show the human and physical features you can see in each photograph.

Picture	Name of place	Location	Human features	Physical features
1				
2				
3				
4				
5				
6				

Which two places were the **most similar** in terms of **physical features**?

_____   _____

Which two places were the **most similar** in terms of **human features**?

_____   _____

Which two places were the **most different** in terms of **physical features**?

_____   _____

Which two places were the **most different** in terms of **human features**?

_____   _____

WATER AND ITS EFFECTS ON THE LANDSCAPE: **Coasts**
Why does this coastline look like this? Page 64

PHOTOCOPIABLE

Name _____   Date _____

Processes of erosion

Bays and headlands are found where different types of rock come into contact with the sea. Some rock is harder, and more resistant to attack from the sea and the processes of erosion, than other rock. So hard rocks usually stick out as cliffs and headlands, while the softer rocks are worn away more quickly, to form bays.

Experiment 1 Look at the different rocks given to you by the teacher (Sample A).
Can you name any of them?
Which do you think are hard rocks?
Which do you think are soft rocks?

Experiment 2 Look at the next sample of stones and rocks (Sample B).
Which stones and rocks have come from a beach?
How can you tell? _____

Coasts can be worn away (eroded) in many ways:
1 Waves, driven on by the wind, break against the base of cliffs, forcing air to be compressed in cracks in the rocks. This weakens the cliff and makes it easier for the sea to wear it away. Occasionally, the pieces of rock just shatter. This is called hydraulic action.
2 Sometimes, in rough seas, the waves are so strong and powerful that they pick up rocks and pebbles and smash them against the bottom of the cliff. This is called abrasion. This process sometimes causes pieces of the cliff to break off and a notch may be formed.
3 Some rocks, like limestone and chalk, may dissolve in water. The joints in the rock may be widened by this process of solution as well as by abrasion. Brine water (salt water) undergoes chemical reactions with many rocks and minerals.
4 Water freezing in crevices expands and breaks off pieces of rock. This is called freeze/thaw action and is caused by ice and frost.
5 Alternating heat and cold causes rocks to expand and contract, and so they become weakened and finally break.
6 The roots of plants grow into crevices, splitting off pieces of rock as they become larger.

Experiment 3 What does acid rain do to rocks?
Stand a small piece of limestone or chalk in vinegar. Watch what happens.
What gas is given off?
How long does it take for the chalk or limestone to completely disappear?

Experiment 4 What does frost do to rocks?
Fill a small plastic bottle *completely* with water and screw the stopper on *tightly*. Leave the bottle in the deep-freeze overnight.
What has happened to the bottle the next day?
Why has this happened?

Experiment 5 What does frost do to saturated rock?
Take small pieces of sandstone, chalk and limestone that have been soaked in water overnight, so the rock is completely saturated and cannot hold any more water. Place the pieces of rock on a small tray and put them in the deep-freeze overnight.
What has happened to the rock the next day?

WATER AND ITS EFFECTS ON THE LANDSCAPE: **Coasts**

PHOTOCOPIABLE   What are these coastal features called? Page 66

Name _____   Date _____

How erosion leads to coastal features

Look at this field sketch of a piece of coastline. Label all the features you can.

This series of drawings shows how a stack is formed.

WATER AND ITS EFFECTS ON THE LANDSCAPE: **Coasts**

What is this coastal settlement like? Page 67

Name _____   Date _____

Coastal settlements research

Name of settlement: _____

Where is this coastal settlement located?	
Name the sea that the place is situated by.	
Describe the landscape.	
What is the climate like in this place?	
What is the function of this coastal settlement? For example, is it a seaside resort, a port, a ferry terminal, a fishing port, or perhaps several of these things?	
What is the size of the settlement in terms of population and area?	
What are the main land-uses? For example, is land used for houses, hotels, tourism, wildlife, a port, farming, industry, leisure, commerce and so on?	
What is the settlement like? List different features, such as houses, shops, hotels, restaurants, industrial areas, port facilities, leisure facilities, tourist attractions and so on. Which features are there most of?	
Does one feature dominate this coastal settlement? If yes, what is it? Is it a physical or a human feature?	
What facilities does the settlement have? What variety of things can you do there? For example, can you live there, work there, go out for a meal or drink, go shopping, spend a holiday, go to a museum, go to the theatre?	
What forms of transport does this settlement have?	
Are there any environmental concerns or issues?	
Make notes of any additional information on the back of this sheet.	

PHOTOCOPIABLE

WATER AND ITS EFFECTS ON THE LANDSCAPE: Coasts
Where do people go on holiday? Page 69

Name _____ Date _____

Client profile cards

Client type 1: Family Beach Holiday
- South coast
- Accommodation: permanent caravan site with entertainment and swimming pool, located right next to beach
- Access to theme park and other attractions necessary

Client type 2: Family Beach Holiday
- Wales
- Accommodation: holiday cottage located right next to beach
- Access to bicycle hire and pony-trekking essential

Client type 3: Family Beach Holiday
- East coast
- Accommodation: hotel right next to beach
- Access to historic houses and castles important

Client type 4: Family Beach Holiday
- Somerset
- Accommodation: apartments on-site with entertainment and a swimming pool, located right next to beach
- Golf course desirable

Client type 5: Holiday for Keen Bird Watchers
- Norfolk coast
- Accommodation: small quiet hotel

Client type 6: Holiday for Disabled and Senior Citizens
- Anywhere on coast, but needs to be on the flat and accessible to wheelchairs
- Accommodation: small quiet hotel

Client type 7: Holiday for Keen Walkers and Mountain Climbers
- Wales or Scotland – on coast
- Accommodation: campsite
- Easy access to mountains to climb

Client type 8: Holiday for Young People
- Anywhere on coast
- Accommodation: apartment
- Water sports, swimming, discos, restaurants

Client type 9: Holiday for Admirers of Scenery
- Anywhere
- Accommodation: good quality hotel, good food

Client type 10: Holiday for People Without a Car
- Coach tour – anywhere on coast
- Accommodation: Good standard of hotel, entertainment in the evening, organised excursions included

Client type 11: Holiday for Keen Sailors
- South coast
- Accommodation: apartment on marine development
- Mooring included. Access to good quality gift shops desirable

Client type 12: Activity Holiday for Teenagers
- Coastal location
- Accommodation: campsite
- Rock climbing, canoeing, surfing, sail boarding, and so on

PRIMARY FOUNDATIONS: Geography: Ages 9–11

WATER AND ITS EFFECTS ON THE LANDSCAPE: Coasts

Where do people go on holiday? Page 69

PHOTOCOPIABLE

Name _____   Date _____

Holiday-maker cards

Hello. My name is Robin Bird. My hobby is watching birds. When I go on holiday I like to be able to take long walks, preferably along a coastal path, and watch birds. I am very interested in rare birds and know that some of the estuaries are visited by rare birds.	Hello. I'm Ron Thorn. I would like a holiday for myself and my good lady wife in a quiet seaside resort. I have a small sailing boat, and my wife likes pottering in gift shops. We would like a comfortable hotel with a balcony and a sea view. We do like the south-west coast – Devon or Cornwall.	Hello. My husband George and myself would like to book a coach tour, visiting a couple of different resorts during our ten-day holiday. We like to take part in organised tours and enjoy the company of others. We like good hotels that offer evening entertainment.
Hello. I'm David and this is my wife Janet. We have two children – Nathan (6) and Wendy (4). We want a holiday with lots for the children to do. We'd like to stay in a caravan right by a nice beach, where there is entertainment. We have a car, so we'd like to be within driving distance of a theme park, a zoo and a craft centre.	Hi! My name is Damien. I am 19 years old and a student at university. A group of four of us would like to book a holiday that is action-packed and fun. We like rock climbing, surfing and water skiing. We also want a resort that is lively at night, with restaurants and discos.	Hello. My name is Mr Wasteach. I am a retired teacher. I would like a quiet holiday by the sea. I don't want to be surrounded by lots of families and children. I want to stay in a small friendly hotel. I like to paint and walk.
Good day. My name is Mr Thomas. I am 80. My wife, who is 78, and I would like to take a short break on the coast. We live in Chester, and don't have a car. We would like to take quite a short train journey to our holiday destination. We would like to stay in a hotel right on the promenade, in a resort that is not full of young families or teenagers.	Hello. Janet and myself have just finished college and haven't much money. We want to do some walking and climbing. We would like some reasonable accommodation in a small seaside town, but with good access to hills and mountains.	Hi! My name is Sarah and I am 13 years old. My parents have said I can go pony-trekking for my holiday this year. I am looking for a good stable with good rides. I enjoy the seashore and the company of others who are into horses.
Hi, my name is Chloe. I'm 16 years old and I'm going on holiday with my younger sister, Mary (10) and my Dad. We want a seaside resort that can offer us all something. Dad likes playing golf, Mary likes swimming and I like water sports. We want to stay in an apartment overlooking the sea.	Hi. My name is Jean. My husband and I would like to book a holiday for ourselves and our three grandchildren (aged 5, 9 and 12). We would like to book into a hotel complex where there is a lot for the children to do, preferably in supervised groups.	Hello. My name is Jenny. I am the Scout leader. I am looking for a holiday for twelve scouts (aged 10 to 14). It must be a very active holiday, with lots of physical things to do. We would like to camp and have our own tents.

PHOTOCOPIABLE

SETTLEMENTS: **Investigating settlements**
What different types of settlements are there? Page 74

Name _____   Date _____

Features of settlements

Name of settlement: _____

Look at the evidence you have about the settlement. Tick the words in the right-hand column that apply to this settlement.

What are the main features of this settlement?	○ homes ○ remains of a castle ○ shops and services ○ cattle market ○ crossing point of a river ○ restaurants ○ industrial estates ○ farm ○ churches ○ leisure centre ○ cinema ○ harbour ○ market square ○ port ○ town hall ○ other (please list) _____
Does this place have few or many features?	○ none ○ few ○ a reasonable variety ○ many
What variety of things can you do in this settlement?	○ live here ○ go shopping ○ see a film or play ○ go to high school ○ go to the leisure centre ○ go for a meal or drink ○ get a job making things or delivering ○ other (please list) _____
Where are the main residential areas?	○ centre of settlement ○ village location ○ edge of settlement ○ remote rural areas
Where are the main shopping areas?	○ centre of settlement ○ edge of settlement ○ other village location (no shopping areas, have to visit other settlements) ○ remote rural area (no shopping areas, have to visit other settlements)
Where are the main industrial areas?	○ centre of settlement ○ edge of settlement (possibly on a 'bypass' road) ○ village location (no industrial areas) ○ remote rural area (no industrial areas)
Is there a dominant feature?	○ yes ○ no if yes, what is it? _____
What type of settlement is this?	○ an isolated dwelling ○ hamlet ○ village ○ town ○ city ○ conurbation ○ other: _____
Why did you put the settlement in this category?	○ variety of services ○ lack of services ○ market charter ○ leisure facilities ○ schools, college, university ○ good local transport ○ settlement serves people from other settlements ○ industrial areas ○ sells things you cannot buy in your own settlement ○ other reasons

Name _____   Date _____

Site and function of settlements

Key characteristics of settlement sites

Characteristic of site	Locate and name two examples
Defensive sites often found on hills or in the loop of a river bend – easy to defend against attacks from enemies	
Bridging points good sites for settlements – rivers could only be crossed where it was possible to build a bridge	
Wet-point sites next to streams or springs – water was essential	

Key functions of settlements

Function	Locate and name two examples
Market towns	
Ports are places where goods can be brought into the country or sent to other countries by ship	
Fishing ports are places where boats bring in their catch	
Ferry ports are where ferries pick up and put down passengers	
Seaside resorts are places where people go for a holiday by the sea	
Industrial centres mainly grow up around factories or mines	
Administration centres are involved in running a large area, such as a county	

PHOTOCOPIABLE

Name _____ Date _____

Economic activities of a settlement

Name of settlement: _____

Look at the evidence you have about the settlement. Use highlighter pens to show which words in the right-hand column apply to this settlement and add any others you can think of.

Primary activities (take it)	Farming: Horticulture: Mining: Other:	mixed, arable, dairy, pigs, sheep, chickens, other (list) vegetables, flowers coal, metal ores, minerals _____ _____
Secondary activities (make it)	Manufacturing industries	_____ _____ _____
Tertiary activities (sell it)	Medical services: Emergency services: Education: Financial services: Legal services: Shops: Leisure facilities: Transport facilities:	doctor, dentist, optician, hospital fire, police primary schools, high schools, colleges, universities banks, building societies, estate agents solicitors, advice centres _____ _____ _____ _____ bus station, railway station, car parks, garages

Name _____   Date _____

Amenities found in a village and in a town

Amenity	Village	Town
Transport Bus services to other larger settlements Trains	1 bus per day – leaves 8.18am returns 4.15pm no train service	buses every 20 mins from 6.30am until 11.00pm main line station, trains every 15 mins
Supermarkets and food shops	no supermarket 1 combined general store, newsagent and post office	3 medium-sized supermarkets
Other shops	1 craft shop, 1 farm shop	25 shops (wide variety of goods sold: clothes, furniture, books, gift shops etc)
Hairdressers	none, but Mrs Turner runs a 'mobile' hairdressing business. She goes to her clients' homes	1 ladies' hairdresser 1 men's hairdresser 2 unisex hairdressers
Cafes, restaurants and pubs	2 pubs	3 pubs, 4 restaurants and 1 café
Post office, banks and building societies	1 combined general store, newsagent and post office	1 post office 3 banks 2 building societies
Libraries	none (mobile library once a fortnight)	1, open 6 days a week, 9am to 8pm
Churches	1 church	2 churches and 1 synagogue
Health services	1 doctor's surgery (open 3 times a week)	1 medical practice (open 5 days a week)
Schools	1 primary school	1 primary school, 1 high school, 1 college
Sports facilities	village football and cricket field golf course keep-fit classes, dance and badminton run in village hall once a week	sports centre (swimming/badminton/football, squash, dance, keep-fit, gym) bowling alley dance studio fitness centre and leisure club tennis club cricket club football club
Play areas	1, with limited amount of play equipment, but lots of open space	1 with limited amount of play equipment 2 that are well-equipped
Garages	none	1 petrol station 1 service centre (repairs and MOTs) 2 combined petrol and repair garages

PHOTOCOPIABLE

Name _____   Date _____

It's all in the name!

Place names help us to find out something about the origin of settlements. They can tell us when the settlement received its name and who named it. Sometimes the name tells us a little about what the landscape was like before the settlement was formed.

Celtic
before AD400

place name endings	meaning
-don/-pen	hill
-coed/-cet	wood
-aber/-inver	mouth of
-perth/-porth	harbour
-caer	fortress
-tre/-bail/-pet	hamlet/ homestead/ village

Scandinavian (Danes and Norse)
AD800–1100

place name endings	meaning
-beck	stream
-by	village
-gate	road
-kirk	church
-thorp	daughter settlement
-thwaite	forest clearing or meadow
-car	marsh

Roman
AD43–450

place name endings	meaning
-caster -chester -cester	city or fortified place
-port	gate, harbour
-street	paved way

Anglo-Saxon
AD450–1100

place name endings	meaning
-ing	territory of the people of
-ham	homestead
-ton	hedged enclosure
-wick	a dairy farm
-ley -worth	clearing in a wood
-bury -borough	fortified place
-den -dene	pasture for pigs in wood
-bridge	bridge
-ford	ford

● Do a place name survey of your own area.
What does the survey tell you about your area when it was first settled?
Who were the main settlers?
● Do a place name survey of another area of the UK.

SETTLEMENTS: **Using television to support the study of settlements**
What types of settlements are there in our home region? Page 84
PHOTOCOPIABLE

Name _____ Date _____

All kinds of settlements

Locate each settlement on maps. Use other sources of information to find out about the settlement. Write your findings in the boxes below. The first box has been filled in as an example.

Name of settlement: Chester **Shape:**

Size (use an Ordnance Survey map): 9 km^2

Function: Defensive site in the past

Type of settlement: City

My question: What are the main economic activities today?

Name of settlement: _____ **Shape:**

Size (use an Ordnance Survey map): _____

Function: _____

Type of settlement: _____

My question: _____

_____

Name of settlement: _____ **Shape:**

Size (use an Ordnance Survey map): _____

Function: _____

Type of settlement: _____

My question: _____

_____

PHOTOCOPIABLE

SETTLEMENTS: **Using television to support the study of settlements**
What are these settlements like? Page 86

Name _____   Date _____

Learning about settlements

Look at the photographs of some settlements in the UK. In the table, write down what the photographs tell you about each settlement.

Settlement	What does the photograph tell me?
Birmingham	_____
Solihull	_____
Tenby	_____
Milford Haven	_____
Barrow	_____
Sheffield	_____
Appleby	_____
Bradford	_____

Think of three questions about these settlements that you'd like to find out about. Write them here.

WHERE? WHY? WHEN? HOW?

1 _____

2 _____

3 _____

SETTLEMENTS: **Using television to support the study of settlements**

How and why do settlements change? Page 87

PHOTOCOPIABLE

Name _____   Date _____

All change!

Which settlements are we learning
about today?

_____

Shops	Housing	Leisure facilities
People who live here	Environmental issues	Land-uses
Jobs people do	Size of settlement	Other changes

PHOTOCOPIABLE

ENVIRONMENTAL CHANGE: Sustainability 'through the window'
What is sustainable development? Page 94

Name _____   Date _____

Every little helps!

It is important to think about how your actions affect the environment.

Look at the table below, which shows the key themes of Agenda 21.

What could you do to help your local authority reach it's target for each theme?

Theme	What could I do?
transport	
energy	
water	
air pollution	
waste	
wildlife	
landscape	

Name _____   Date _____

What can you see through the window?

Write down three adjectives to describe what the picture shows.

1 _____ 2 _____ 3 _____

Write a sentence to describe how the picture makes you feel.

_____

_____

_____

PHOTOCOPIABLE

ENVIRONMENTAL CHANGE: Sustainability 'through the window'
What is sustainable transport? Page 95

Name _____   Date _____

Getting there!

Travelling by bike, by foot and by public transport causes less damage to the environment than travelling by car. Cycling, walking and public transport are more **sustainable modes of transport**.

1 Working in pairs, produce a questionnaire to find out how other children get to school.

● It *does not* need to be long.
● It *does* need to be quick and easy to fill in.

Use these headings to help you:

age	driving	weather
distance	walking	cost
transport	cycling	safety

2 Test your questionnaire out on your partner. What have you found out?

_____

_____

3 Now ask other children to complete your questionnaire.

The facts you collect will help you to think about how you could encourage more people to use sustainable modes of transport (cycling, walking, public transport).
What could you do around your school and local area?

_____

_____

_____

Name _____   Date _____

Through the window – a more sustainable future

PHOTOCOPIABLE

ENVIRONMENTAL CHANGE: **What happens to all that waste?**
What do we throw away? Page 103

Name _____   Date _____

What's in rubbish?

We all create waste and throw all sorts of things into our dustbins. Waste is created everywhere – at home, at school, in factories and in offices. Every year, each one of us throws away about ten times our own weight in household rubbish!

1 Design a data collection sheet and carry out a simple 'rubbish' survey at lunchtime in school.
2 Think about the origins of some of the rubbish.
3 Think about what the pieces of rubbish are made of.
4 Analyse the data you have collected, using a spreadsheet package (draw graphs, pie charts, and so on).

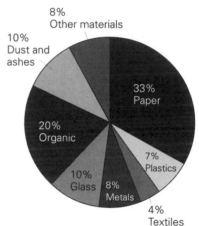

This chart gives the percentage (by weight) of each type of material found in the average UK dustbin.

5 How might the percentage by weight of waste be different from the percentage by volume? (Think about things like plastic bottles.)

_____

_____

In the UK, every year we throw away:

Item	Number
Glass containers (bottles and jars)	6000 million
'PET' plastic bottles (PET is a type of plastic used for soft drinks bottles)	1100 million
Batteries	500 million
Drinks cans	5500 million
Food cans	4000 million
Other cans	200 million

6 In groups, discuss the data above, and consider what actions each one of us could take to reduce the amount of rubbish we produce.

_____

_____

PHOTOCOPIABLE

Name _____   Date _____

Waste not, want not

100 FINISH	99 Buy individual servings of butter, **move back 6 places**	98	97 Buy a new computer with lots of packaging, **move back 5 places**	96 Drop litter in the school playground, **miss a go**	95 Buy goods that don't have a lot of useless packaging, **move on 3 places**	94 Help your grandparents take their empty glass bottles to a bottle bank, **move on 4 places**	93	92	91 Put glass bottles in the bin, **miss a go**
81	82 Sort your cans into ones that can be recycled and ones which can't, **move on 2 places**	83	84	85 Put potato peelings on the compost heap, **move on 3 places**	86	87 Buy envelopes made of recycled paper, **move on 2 places**	88 BOTTLE BANK	89 BOTTLE BANK	90 At school, start a compost heap in the garden, **have another go**
80	79	78	77 Drop litter in the park, **miss a go**	76 Start to collect aluminium foil, **have another go**	75	74	70	72 Use your local aluminium can bank, **move on 3 places**	71
61	62	63 Buy individual servings of jam, **move back 2 places**	64	65 Use your local bottle bank, **move on 4 places**	66	67	68 Help your neighbours start a compost heap in their garden, **have another go**	69	70
60 Drop litter in the town centre, **miss a go**	59	58 Put your old newspapers in your local paper bank, **move on 3 places**	57	56	55 Buy fresh fruit without any packaging, **move on 4 places**	54	53	52	51 Give good shoes you have outgrown to a charity shop, **have another go**
41	42	43	44 Buy recycled writing paper, **move on 2 places**	45	46	47 Use your local recycling centre, **move on 5 places**	48	49 At school, organise a class project to collect aluminium cans, **have another go**	50
40	39	38 Buy a new CD player with lots of packaging, **move back 4 places**	37	36	35 Use your local textile bank, **move on 2 places**	34	33 Give a good toy you are too old to play with to a charity shop, **have another go**	32	31 Start a compost heap in the garden, **have another go**
21	22	23 Put returnable milk bottles in the dustbin, **miss a go**	24	25	26 Give good clothes that you have outgrown to a charity shop, **move on 3 places**	27	28	29	30 Give unwanted toys to a jumble sale, **have another go**
20	19	18 Refuse a carrier bag at the supermarket, **move on 2 places**	17	16	15	14 Return your plastic carrier bags to the supermarket, **move on 2 places**	13	12	11
1 START	2 Buy milk in returnable bottles, **move on 4 places**	3 Buy a bottle of perfume with lots of packaging, **miss a go**	4 Start to collect aluminium cans, **have another go**	5 Buy fresh vegetables without any packaging, **move on 4 places**	6	7	8 Throw good clothes that you have outgrown into the dustbin, **miss 2 goes**	9	10 Throw old books in quite good condition in the dustbin, **miss a go**

PHOTOCOPIABLE

Name _____ Date _____

Visit to the landfill site

Although I already knew that

I have learnt some new facts from our visit to the landfill site. I learnt that

I also learned that

Another fact I learned is

But the most interesting thing I learned was

Name _____   Date _____

On the scrap heap

Recycling in economically less developed countries

Sketch of article	What is it?	How has it been made?	Who made it?	What is it used for?	Country

PHOTOCOPIABLE

ENVIRONMENTAL CHANGE: What happens to all that waste?
Where shall we build a new landfill site? Page 110

Name _____   Date _____

Another landfill site? Not in our locality!

Mrs Upset, Local resident Why should this area be chosen for a landfill site? It will make the value of my house go down. We will also be plagued with rats and flies in the summer and birds scavenging and spreading diseases.

Mr Teach, Headteacher of local primary school I am very concerned because there will be an increase in heavy lorries passing the school. Many children walk or cycle to school and this increase in traffic will increase the dangers to the children. We teach our children to be responsible citizens and think about the impact of rubbish on the world, not just our local area. That is why we try to follow the '4 Rs'

Mr Shoppingham, Local newsagent and village shopkeeper The extra traffic will generate extra trade for my shop. I will probably start to do cups of tea, all day breakfasts and fast microwave food. It will keep the shop open, so locals can still use it. If I don't increase trade, I may have to close.

Mr Growton, Local farmer We don't want a landfill site here. If it isn't managed properly, our land will become contaminated and polluted and our crops will fail. Even if the land doesn't become contaminated, our customers will think it might be and avoid buying our produce. Our lives will be ruined and our land worth nothing.

Mrs Fillit, Director of 'Dig a Hole Landfill Co. Ltd.' This is the absolute perfect site. The soil is clay, the roads are wide enough to be used by the lorries and the site is only overlooked by three houses. The farmer doesn't produce anything on this piece of land and he is keen to sell it to us. After the site is full, we will landscape the area and make it into a recreational facility for the public.

Mr Planit, Independent Consultant and Engineer I have done a survey on this land for the local council and, with the local planning office, have drawn up some plans for the landfill development. I believe this is an ideal site, because of the underlying geology and the soil type.

Ms Voteforme, Local Councillor This development will be good for the area. It will create extra employment for local people and earn extra money for the council. The land is very boggy, being clay soil, and is difficult to farm. This will make good use of a poor piece of land.

Miss Industson, Group of Industrialists I represent some of the local industrialists. My members think the landfill development is a good idea. We will be able to dispose of our waste on the managed landfill site and this will help stop our waste – sometimes hazardous waste – from polluting the land, rivers, lakes and seas.

Miss Saveit, Environmentalist This is an area designated as a Site of Special Scientific Interest (SSSI). A very rare orchid grows here on the clay soil. The creation of a landfill site will destroy this plant and also destroy the habitat of many animals and birds.

Mr Concerned, Local resident I have lived here all my life but am very concerned about this proposed landfill site. I have done a lot of reading about landfill sites, and even though I realise they are needed – because we all produce too much waste – I just do not want one here. Perhaps if we all followed the actions of the local primary school children and adopted their 'Refuse, Re-use, Recycle, Reduce' slogan there would be no need for so many landfill sites.

Tom, Local child I live in one of the houses that would overlook the proposed landfill site. My mum is very upset about this. She says our house won't be worth the amount of money we have paid for it and that we won't be able to sell it. She is very concerned about the health risks to my baby brother and me.

Mr Sellit, Local farmer who owns the land That piece of land is no good for farming. It is clay soil and always wet and boggy. I cannot grow anything on it or graze my animals there. If I sell the land to the landfill company, I will be able to give up farming and retire.